"This is a beautiful book, honest and tender and wise. In its own lyrical way, it is also a call to action. Grandmothers such as Marty Norman may be our salvation yet."

—TIM MADIGAN
author of *I'm Proud of You: My Friendship with Fred Rogers*

"Marty Norman is the grandmother we all wish we'd had. Her book offers hope, strength, and wisdom without any preachiness for a new generation of savvy, sophisticated women who are a bit surprised to be happily answering to names such as Nana, Mimi, and Marme. The rendering of her journey of faith during these grandmothering years cuts through the stereotypes and offers a fresh look at the bonds that can be forged between grandparents and the kids' kids."

—PRUDENCE MACKINTOSH
author of *Retreads* and
Thundering Sneakers

"Marty Norman captures the shear joy of being a grandmother as she shares that being a grandmother is the only thing in life that is not overrated. It is a grand opportunity to love, to share, and to give unconditionally. Marty shares her wisdom and reminds us what a great gift grandmothering is."

—U.S. CONGRESSWOMAN
KAY GRANGER
grandmother of three

"Grandmothers, gray or not, will delight in this great book filled with warm stories, fresh insight, and new reasons to go hug their own darlings! Marty has captured the joy and wonder that only grandmothers know. Enjoy! Be blessed!"

—JAN SILVIOUS
author of *Smart Girls Think Twice* and *Big Girls Don't Whine*

"As a baby-boomer grandma, I found myself slapping high-fives and jumping into the air (not too high!) to click my heels as I read Marty Norman's exciting new book, *Generation G*. What a long-awaited and much-needed breath of fresh air! I'm a grandmother of nine who doesn't apologize for (or lie about) my age, who dotes on my exceptionally brilliant and adorable grandchildren, and yet still enjoys riding on the back of my husband's Harley. Marty gives us permission to grow old with class and finesse, to enjoy (and maybe even spoil) our grandkids, and to impart a little experience and wisdom along the way. In a warm, fireside-chat manner, she speaks to us baby-boomer grandparents right where we're at—and we relate and appreciate that she helps us maneuver through yet another changing season of life."

—KATHI MACIAS
author of *Beyond Me: Living a You-First Life in a Me-First World*

"*Stop the presses!* Trust me . . . this is also a great book for grandfathers who are gray, bald, and not nearly as savvy as our counterparts!"

—RON HALL
aka "Rocky Pop" to three little granddaughters and author of *Same Kind of Different as Me*

GENERATION

GENERATION

G

ADVICE FOR
SAVVY GRANDMOTHERS
WHO WILL NEVER GO GRAY

MARTY NORMAN

THOMAS NELSON
Since 1798

NASHVILLE DALLAS MEXICO CITY RIO DE JANEIRO BEIJING

Published in Nashville, Tennessee, by Thomas Nelson. Thomas Nelson is a trademark of Thomas Nelson, Inc.

Thomas Nelson, Inc. titles may be purchased in bulk for educational, business, fund-raising, or sales promotional use. For information, please e-mail SpecialMarkets@ThomasNelson.com.

Unless otherwise noted, Scripture quotations are taken from the Holy Bible, New International Version®. Copyright 1973, 1978, 1984 by International Bible Society. Used by permission of Zondervan Bible Publishing House. All rights reserved.

Scripture quotations marked NASB are taken from the New American Standard Bible®, © The Lockman Foundation 1960, 1962, 1963, 1968, 1971, 1972, 1973, 1975, 1977, 1995. Used by permission.

Scripture quotations marked KJV are taken from the Holy Bible, King James Version.

Reference in Chapter 25 is taken from the *NIV Life Application Bible* (Grand Rapids: Zondervan, 2005), 2262 (note on 1 Peter 3:11).

"Do You Hear What I Hear?" by Noel Regney and Gloria Shayne ©1962. Jewel Music Publishing Co., Inc. All rights reserved.

"The Gambler" © 1977 Sony/ATV Tunes LLC. All rights administered by Sony/ATV Music Publishing, 8 Music Square West, Nashville, TN 37203. All rights reserved. Used by permission.

Excerpts from "Mrs. Doubtfire" © 1993, courtesy of Twentieth Century Fox. Written by Randi Mayem Singer and Leslie Dixon. All rights reserved.

Library of Congress Cataloging-in-Publication Data

Norman, Marty, 1945–
    Generation G : advice for savvy grandmothers who will never go gray / Marty
Norman.
        p. cm.
    ISBN 978-0-7852-2812-7 (pbk.)
    1. Grandmothers—Religious life. 2. Grandmothers. 3. Aging—Religious aspects—
Chrisitanity. 4. Aging. 5. Norman, Marty, 1945– I. Title.
BV4528.5.N67 2007
248.8085'3—dc22   2007042920

Printed in the United States of America

08 09 10 11 12 RRD 5 4 3 2 1

For . . .

Jim, whose love, support, and commitment in
our marriage have made this book possible;

Lee, whose sweet encouragement brought the
joys of grandparenting into my life;

Darin, whose creative spirit and memory have
encouraged my gifts;

Holly and Blythe, whose addition and presence
complete our family;

Jack, Lily, James, and Strother, who are the lights
of my life—who fill my days with wonder.

This is what the past is for! Every experience God gives us, every person he puts in our lives is the perfect preparation for the future that only he can see.

—CORRIE TEN BOOM AND
ELIZABETH AND JOHN SHERRILL,
The Hiding Place★

★ *ChosenBooks, a Division of Baker Book House, Grand Rapids, 2006.*

CONTENTS

CONTENTS

CONTENTS

ACKNOWLEDGMENTS

First and foremost, I want to thank God for his blessings and the abundance he has showered upon me. I dedicate this book to his glory.

I also want to thank the women in my life whose grandmother roles have forever shaped me: my mother, Frances Gupton; my grandmothers, Frances Morgan, Pauline Seay, and Helen Gupton; my great-grandmother, Martha Van Zandt; and my mother-in-law, Rubye Faye Norman.

I am blessed to have many friends who have woven themselves throughout the seasons of my life. Their friendship, love, support, prayers, and generosity were the fabric that brought this book together. I give thanks to God for all of them.

Much thanks go to the women in my prayer group, the Wednesday Watchmen—Mary Ellen Davenport, Phyliss Dunn, Christy Fonvielle, Lauren Gage, Bobbie Harper, Rosalind Laird, Claire McDermott, Jeannie Ott, Debbie Petta, Candy Rehfeldt, Janina Walker, Belinda Whiddon, and Cathy Womack—for their faithfulness in prayer on my behalf.

Special thanks to the Four Star Coffee Group—Courtney Dickerson, Carolyn Fraley, Carole Petty, and Beverly Snyder—whose openness, sharing, and support have allowed my journey to form over the past ten years.

Last but not least are my dear friends from elementary school, the Bluebirds, with whom I've shared a lifetime—Lucy Brants, Megan Bobbitt, Ambler Cantey, Nona Carmichael, Lynn Farley, Lana Hadlock, Bari Holden, Missy Lawson, Ann McKinney, Gail Moore Wiedner, Carol Presnall, and Barbara Wild.

I am so grateful to friends who have preceded me on the other side of the veil, whose lives impacted me in ways that cannot fully be expressed: Ann Call, Jan Carsey, Deborah Hall, Anita Street, and Diane Taylor.

I also thank the Joy Writers Group, especially Frank Ball, Christy Foneville, and Suzanne Hern, whose encouragement, support, and attention to detail taught me about writing and helped perfect my craft.

I especially want to thank Lenda Richards, whose inspiration of the First Grandmother's Club gave voice to my heart; Jean Giles-Sims, whose friendship and encouragement got me back into writing after a twenty-year hiatus; Suzan Cook, whose artistic expression gave pictures to my words; Mary Ellen Davenport, whose perseverance in prayer moved mountains; Ron Hall, whose friendship and willingness to step out on a limb for me opened doors not even imaginable; and Lucy Brants, who helped translate the content of the book and the legalese of the contract. I also want to thank Debbie Wickwire, my editor and friend, who took a chance on an unknown writer, giving voice to my passion; Jennifer Stair, whose patience and caring attention to detail in copyediting polished my message; and Rhonda Hogan, whose expertise in copyright and permissions kept me on track.

Most importantly, I want to thank my husband, Jim, who tirelessly read each draft of the book, offering advice as well as love and support; my brother, Bill, whose chapter-by-chapter analysis brought unity to the book; my sons, Lee and Darin, my daughters-in-law, Holly and Blythe, and my grandchildren, Jack, Lily, James, and Strother, without whom there would be no book. They have blessed my life immeasurably, and I treasure every way they intersect my world.

INTRODUCTION

THE ESSENCE OF *G*

> Your people will rebuild the ancient ruins and will raise
> up the age-old foundations; you will be called Repairer
> of Broken Walls, Restorer of Streets with Dwellings.
> —Isaiah 58:12

I am now a *grandmother*—a pivotal point in the lives of those I love. Never in my wildest dreams did I think I would find myself in this position. How did I get here? What do I do?

And more importantly, where is the manual?

Like it or not, I am now the matriarch of the family. Not only are my children and grandchildren looking to me for answers, but they also expect me to be a guiding light in a world gone awry, a strong fortress in a battleground of ideologies. As chief caregiver—sandwiched between four generations—I have found that in a short span of time, my responsibilities have multiplied tenfold.

I suspect that most twenty-first-century grandmothers face this same dilemma. We are searching for answers to these questions and trying to overcome our doubts.

I pondered this reality as I approached the birth of my first grandchild. I wondered how his birth would affect my life. After he was born, I was overwhelmed by the answer. The wonder, joy, and love that pour out from me toward my grandchildren are beyond anything I could have ever expected or hoped.

Being a grandmother is the best—it can't be overrated. But this new role comes with a major question: how do I balance my new role as grandmother with the other responsibilities in my life? At sixty, I am placed between my mother and in-laws, my two adult sons and daughters-in-law, and my four grandchildren, who are the lights of my life. My husband runs a business and manages his parents' ranch on the side. I am a part-time bookkeeper, freelance writer, and licensed therapist. My role is to keep our lives in order, which is no easy task as our responsibilities multiply on a daily basis. My husband and I are physically active and love to travel. We even ski, bike, hike, and ride horses on occasion.

I like to think that I keep up. I am technologically savvy and fairly computer literate. I even use e-invites and e-mail. At the same time, I stand firm in the old ways, refusing to give in to call waiting or caller ID.

How does a twenty-first-century grandmother cope with these realities? How do I balance my two feet in four worlds?

The answer is simple. Rather than worrying about the destination, I focus on the journey. As I integrate the responsibilities and joys of grandparenting into my life, I am able to move forward. Accepting the reality that graying is merely a state of mind, I shape my attitude to fit my new role. As I blend the past, present, and future, I place my feet on a solid foundation and become what I believe.

The journey is unavoidable. The good news is that I am prepared. I have a storehouse of experience that is overflowing with supplies for the journey. With the teachings of God and the examples of my mother, grandmothers, and mother-in-law, my own life experiences act as my guide, and I have the opportunity to turn my God-given gifts into a godly influence for my family. What could be more important than that?

All grandmothers are faced with the dilemma of how to leave a legacy for the next generation. Gifted with wisdom, we have the opportunity to pour ourselves out as healers of the generations, repairers of the breach, and peacemakers in a world of chaos. Grandparenting is our consummate opportunity to serve rather than to be served, to love without taking offense, and to cheerlead and hand-hold those who come behind.

As grandmothers, we hold life in the balance, but somewhere in the intervening years we have grown to the task.

The journey is the essence of grandmothers. The destination is the essence of God.

There is no perfect manual for grandparents, only a handbook of shared experience. We each have to find our own way. Our lives have taken different paths, but we share a common desire to love and support our families. Our call is to pass on the wisdom of the ages before our time is finished on earth, in order to make an eternal difference in the lives of those we love.

Generation G is my story—how I am celebrating and coping with the graying of my life. It can be read in one sitting, as individual points of reflection, or topically in times of need.

Each of us has a story. I suspect that, deep down, your story is not all that different from mine. My hope is that as you read these chapters, you will be challenged to apply your own life lessons to your world. My prayer is that by the grace of God, we might plant the seeds of a godly legacy that will reap a bountiful harvest of faith and wisdom for our families. I am confident that each of us will impact our world in a unique way.

We are blessed to be given the gift of grandparenting.

It is a gift to pass on.

PART 1
GRAND TRANSITIONS

ONE

RICH, SAVVY, AND SILVER

For you, O God, tested us; you refined us like silver.
—Psalm 66:10

Let's face it: the twentieth-century grandmother is no more. Gone are the days of shirtwaist dresses, aprons, and rocking chairs. Good-bye to standing hair appointments and the sprayed chignon. Hello to flat irons, mousse, and hair gel. Like it or not, large grocery store chains have replaced homemade pie crust and homegrown tomatoes.

It is a new day. Twenty-first-century grandmothers are a new kind of breed. I know—I am one.

Look around you, and you'll see that baby boomers are changing the face of grandparenting. Many of us have discretionary income and are savvy to the ways of the world. But how does rich, savvy, and silver describe today's grandmother?

The idea came to me one Saturday morning as I was making my weekly run through Target. As I passed by a bright red T-shirt with the words *Rich, Sassy, and Single* emblazoned on the front in iridescent colors, I thought, *Now, that concept is certainly lost on my generation.* Then it hit me: if I created a T-shirt for my generation, I would print the words *Rich, Savvy, and Silver* in much larger letters. That's us. That's my generation. As I went to my car, I continued to ponder from what depth such a profound thought had come.

The meaning soon became clear. These three adjectives are a succinct description of twenty-first-century grandmothers—women who are so abundantly blessed that we have the motivation and ability to give back a hundredfold. Let's briefly consider each of these concepts.

How are we *rich*? We have a wealth of wisdom and life experience. In recent years, my family has nearly tripled in size, yet I still have the time and ability to travel, shop, create, and do many other activities. I often find myself overcome by the abundance of my life. In my lifetime I have seen everything from birth to death, illness to healing, light to dark, happy to sad. My history has made me who I am. I have lost loved ones to accidents or death, sat by the bedside of a dying parent, and helped families deal with alcohol or drug addiction. I have grieved with friends whose homes were devastated by natural disasters. I have felt pain as churches implode and families divide.

I have also been blessed to experience miracles. I have rejoiced as prodigal sons and daughters have returned home. I have seen marriages restored and families reunited. I have witnessed deathbed conversions and experienced healing, forgiveness, sacrificial giving, and generosity beyond understanding.

Yes, my generation has a lot of experience and wisdom to share.

To state the obvious, I am also rich in years. Years of love, laughter, joy, wonder, sadness, trials, and temptations—many years, many lessons. I've seen a lot, from the invention of the television to the landing on the moon, from the computer to the cell phone. I've watched the Berlin Wall come down, the Cuban embargo go up, and the wars in Vietnam, the Gulf, and Iraq. I've watched *Roy Rogers and Dale Evans*, *I Love Lucy,* and *Mission Impossible*.

A lot of years, a lot of life. Our generation is rich indeed.

Defining how we are *savvy* was harder. My thesaurus gives the following as synonyms for *savvy*: shrewd, understanding, discerning. These adjectives describe my generation. We have a shrewd understanding of life. I doubt any of us wants to go back in years, but everything we are today comes from those years of trial and error. Our past affects our future.

We are also multifaceted. We have sung in choirs, been on boards, founded neighborhood associations, rafted rivers, climbed mountains, gone on mission trips, worked with the homeless, taught Sunday school, watched solar eclipses, picnicked in the park, danced on crutches, written poetry, sung songs, cried with friends, laughed with lovers, and lived life to the best of our ability. We have discerned danger and observed corruption. We have learned whom to trust and whom not to trust. We have a pretty good handle on life.

Yes, we are a savvy generation, not easily fooled.

Last but not least, we are *silver*. Ten years ago, I decided to go natural. My hair is as silver as the mane on the Lone Ranger's horse. Sometimes people describe my hair as gray, but I prefer the term *silver*, for I will never grow gray. Gray is a mind-set, a metaphor for growing old, but silver is vibrant and alive, a celebration of life. Silver also connotes hope, an attitude that shines with life, rejoicing in where we have been, where we are now, and where we are going.

But silver is not just a hair color. Silver is a valuable metal that shines, refined to showcase its purity. As the silversmith perfects the metal, he holds it over the hottest part of the fire to burn away the impurities. By the same token, in order for God to refine us, he holds us close to the fire to burn away the dross. Most of us have been through God's refining fire time and again, but as our children are quick to say, our process is not yet complete. Surely we are further along the path than we were yesterday.

So the title of this chapter is perfect, for it describes my generation—Generation G grandmothers who are in process of becoming who we were created to be.

Rich, savvy, and silver. That's me—and I'm proud of it!

TWO

ALL ABOARD

Therefore I tell you, do not worry about your life, what
you will eat; or about your body, what you will wear.
Life is more than food, and the body more than clothes.
—Luke 12:22-23

Transitioning into grandparenting is a journey, much like
riding the train to camp. It takes a long time to get there,
but once you arrive, it's the best.

When I was a little girl, my mother used to tell me, "It's
not the destination but the journey that counts." At the age
of twelve, I took my first train trip away from home to Camp
Nakanawa in Mayland, Tennessee. On that ride, I learned what
she meant.

Accompanied by twenty eager campers, I boarded the

train at the crack of dawn for the two-day ride to Tennessee. As the journey began, I was timid and a little afraid, for I was not sure what to expect. At each stop, as new people boarded the train, my anticipation grew. Girls ran up and down the aisle meeting and greeting one another, and I discovered a larger world that I had never known before. This trip was the beginning of a great adventure.

The journey into grandparenting is a bit like that train ride—filled with uncertainty, excitement, and adventure. The journey has taken us up hills and down valleys, yet we are still chugging along like the Little Engine That Could.

Somewhere along the way, as that twelve-year-old girl became a grandmother of four, I somehow misplaced my enthusiasm and sense of wonder. I'm not sure when it happened, but I know that I am not alone. If we're honest, most women would admit the same has happened to them. We spend the majority of our time racing toward the destination—the wedding, the kids, the new house, college tuition, retirement. Focusing on our goals, we fail to take in the view or learn from the people in our paths. We have forgotten the lessons of childhood. We are far too busy looking toward the destination to enjoy the journey.

Much can be gleaned from this twelve-year-old girl. Just as

she excitedly anticipated the ride, so, too, must we—for once on the train there is no turning back, no getting off.

The best part is that, today, as a grandmother, I have a choice. All is not lost, for I have many different options from which to choose—fast trains, slow trains, or sleek, modern, old-fashioned, or dependable ones. I can change club cars at will. I might visit the dining car and choose from a menu of assorted gourmet or comfort foods. If my body is weary, I might move to the sleeping car for a time of rest or reflection. I can move easily from car to car, from activity to activity, trying out new things, or I can push forward in search of something better.

Either way, I am on the train. And the train is on the move.

Recently my husband, Jim, read about an old-fashioned steam engine that is still making a daily run between Palestine and Rusk, Texas. His great-uncle Houston was a conductor based out of Palestine; therefore, he was eager to ride this train. In addition to reliving the past, he also wanted to fill in some gaps in his family history—a double-blessing opportunity.

Therefore, on a beautiful fall morning with our friends Courtney and Ray in tow, we packed the car and headed south. As we neared Palestine, we were struck by the change in scenery. The hills were green and rolling. The trees were a wheel of color. Farms and pastures dotted the landscape, and the two-lane highway made for a slower, more delightful drive.

Once on the train, we experienced the perfect outing. Ninety minutes each way, plus time for a picnic at a picturesque lake, we found ourselves leaning back, taking in the scenery. We turned our hyper meters down and our imaginations up as we visualized early settlers exploring the forested terrain. We talked and watched and just enjoyed the journey.

Halfway through the trip, our engineer switched to a side track to let an oncoming train pass. I was reminded that this is not unlike my own journey. In my world, there are miles of railroad track. At any moment, the Engineer might switch to a different track. I may not have a say as to which track he will take, what gain or loss I might experience, but I can be assured that he is taking care of me.

I know that my well-being is his utmost concern. It is important to him that I am not alone, for he is careful to place conductors, drivers, brakemen, and passengers alongside me. He stays with me every moment of the ride, until the train pulls into its final destination.

The transition into grandparenting is like the train to Palestine. There is nothing to worry about. If I open my eyes and look, I will experience new vistas. If I stare in wonder at the amazing scenery placed before me, the ride will be filled with surprise and unexpected blessings.

I'm blessed to be on the train with a round-trip ticket. All aboard! Let's get this train on the move.

THREE

MADE TO BE A GRANDMOTHER

[She] is like a tree planted by streams of water, which
yields its fruit in season.

—Psalm 1:3

I was made to be a grandmother—no doubt about it. I love
every aspect of this journey. I love holding that tiny baby,
rocking my grandchild in the wee hours of the morning
until we both fall asleep. I love fixing peanut butter sand-
wiches and picnicking in the yard under the oak tree. I love
searching for rubber ducky, submarines, wash gloves, bath
paint, and empty shampoo bottles under the bubbles in the
bathtub. Most of all, I love the way I feel when my grandchildren say, "I love you."

Being a grandmother is the best. I believe it is the only
thing in life that is not overrated. From the moment my son
walked out of the door holding that little bundle of joy, I was

hooked. I looked at that tiny miracle, thanked God, and said to my grandson, "Welcome to the world. We have been waiting for you!" I felt the same way with each birth. My favorite pictures are the ones of my sons, taken moments after each of their babies were born. The looks on their faces makes me cry to this day.

It was not hard to learn how to be a grandmother. I knew instinctively what to do. I reached down into my heart, and love poured out of me toward my grandchildren. Each year has just gotten better. I love discovering life with each of my grandchildren. I love their unique personalities. I love discovering more about myself as I spend time with them. I love singing silly songs and dancing the Hokey Pokey. I even love their endless questions (most of the time!). No, grandparenting has not been hard.

What has been hard is figuring out how best to relate to my grown children as a grandparent. There is so much I want to tell them, so much wisdom and experience I want to share. But I realize that just as when I was a young mother, they need to find their own way. My journey has been uniquely mine, and so, too, shall theirs. It is hard, but I am learning to keep my mouth shut. I am learning from the examples of my own grandmothers and their interactions with my family.

My mother tells a story about her grandmother, Gangy, who came to live with my mother's family when she was widowed at the age of fifty. My mother says life was wonderful with Gangy in the house. She offered encouragement and help, yet she never interfered with the family. Every night after dinner she went upstairs to her room to give the family time together.

Gangy was a true lady. A schoolteacher in the early 1900s, she traveled to Fort Worth in a covered wagon, yet she kept up an active lifestyle until her death at ninety-five. She loved to watch *Meet the Press* and could argue politics and religion with the best, yet she made her point in a gentle, soft-spoken way. I used to sit with Gangy in the kitchen as she gave herself an insulin shot for her diabetes, never complaining about it. There, perched atop a kitchen stool, she regaled me with tales of her childhood.

Although Gangy was physically gray-headed, she was silver in spirit, spiritually and emotionally full of life. She was connected to the world, but more importantly, she made an impact on everyone she knew. This is how I want to be.

I adored both of my grandmothers. One died too young, and the other I enjoyed until I was twenty-four. I still remember how much they adored me. They were an integral part of my life. Much of who I am today comes from the lessons I learned at their feet.

Yes, I love being a grandmother. I come from a long line of them. It suits me well.

FOUR

THE CYCLE OF LIFE

There is a time for everything, and a season for every
activity under heaven.

—Ecclesiastes 3:1

The cycle of life has a funny way of coming around again
and again. If you live long enough, you will begin to see
things reemerge. There is a certain circular motion to life—
truly a time and season for all generations.

As grandmothers, we are blessed to be witnesses to such
cycles. If we open our eyes, if we listen with our ears and
our hearts, we begin to see the divine appointments that
bring healing and wholeness to families. This resolution often
occurs in the later years, sometimes through an experience
of grief or even the process of dying. Either way, resolution
acts as a healing balm to cleanse our spirits. Often through

circumstances we cannot even begin to understand, we find opportunities for healing.

One thing I know for certain: I want to be an agent of healing. I want to allow the cycle of life to regenerate within, through, and around me, as my own life begins the final healing process. I want to be an effective healer in my family, to deal with my own issues as they resurface and beg to be healed. I want to come into my own fullness.

It is as it should be. It is as God intended. We are born, we live, and we die. Yet in between these stages there are myriad life experiences, moments of truth, and divine appointments.

I am now in the fall season of life's cycle, three-fourths of the way around the circle. I love the fall. The air is crisp and fresh. The light falls on the leaves as they dance with light. I love the colors of fall, unique but perfect in their beauty. Days are shorter, but the sunsets are magnificent. The October sky is as clear and blue and perfect as any other season. Winter is approaching but has not yet arrived.

Fall is a good time.

I like to think that like the fall season, I dance with light, that I radiate and reflect that which I have come to be and believe. I want to be a crisp breath of fresh air to those who are weary from the heat of summer. I hope I am clear in my thinking and my colors are shining through in my behavior. I pray that as my sun sets, I reflect the clouds about me and shine with all the colors of the rainbow. I like to think that although my leaves are falling, I am dealing with their loss with grace and integrity. I pray my hopes and dreams will germinate and fertilize next year's growth.

I like that I am fall. I want to take advantage of the opportunity placed before me to prepare for winter, but I also desire to breathe life upon the coming spring. I look forward to time with my grandchildren . . . whispering with them quietly in the night . . . telling stories of spaceships and circuses . . . building make-believe houses of sheets and pillows . . . listening and laughing and sharing as only a grandmother can do.

Yes, I like fall. I like being in a place where I can plant seeds for the coming spring. I like to breathe healing upon the generations. I hope my children and grandchildren will believe that this was my best season. I pray that when their times come, they will step into their own fall with great anticipation.

It is as it should be—the cycle of life is moving on, and I am moving with it.

FIVE

DAY BY DAY

Seek the LORD while he may be found;
call on him while he is near.
—Isaiah 55:6

A A and Al-Anon have a saying: "One day at a time." I like these words because they speak truth. Today is reality. The present is all we have. When times are tough, we only have to step out one hour, one minute at a time. We need only put one foot in front of the other.

In his book, *Practicing the Presence of God*, Brother Lawrence expands upon this "one day at a time" philosophy. In every aspect of his life, this humble seventeenth-century monk practiced living in the present moment. While walking, washing the dishes, or doing his chores, he moved in the now, seeing God in all things. He learned the art of being present. We can learn a lot from Brother Lawrence.

Before I became a grandmother, I had no idea how to live in the present. Too involved with the future, I dreaded what might happen. Too preoccupied with the past, I regretted lost opportunities. I spent much of my time holding onto grudges or wishing for different results. I can say from experience that living in the past or the future does not add one minute more to one's life. In fact, it distracts from experiencing the now.

It was not until I went to Montserrat that I began to have an inkling of how to practice the present moment. Montserrat is a retreat center I have attended for the past fifteen years. Every year for four days, I go on a silent retreat, fasting from the world. The constant bombardment of the world and the noise pollution of radio and TV overstimulate me, distracting me from living in the now. It is only in the silence that I began to appreciate the moment. Often it is not until I am totally removed from the world that I begin to see the hand of God.

I can attest that, as the saying goes, when I suit up, he shows up.

My first memory of experiencing the moment occurred at Montserrat. I was sitting on a bench, trying to reconcile a conflict in my marriage. In front of me was a large tree. Interspersed with its green, perfectly shaped branches were long, bare branches resembling scarecrow arms. I couldn't imagine what kind of tree this was. Not until I moved to a different spot on the bench did I realize I was actually looking at two trees, one directly in front of the other. At that moment, I was presented with truth. Position affects perception; perception affects perspective. I was able to look at my own situation in a new light. My conflict became clearer because I had changed my position. Looking at the conflict from another perspective, I was astounded by what I saw.

At the same retreat, I also discovered prayer. Though I had prayed for many years, my prayers had been more like demands, petitions that screamed, "Give me, give me, give me!" I am sure God smiled and just shook his head. I didn't realize that prayer is a two-way communication. When I quit doing all the talking, when I take time to reflect in silence, I get answers to my questions. God is ready to reveal himself to me, but not until I am present in the now can I fully experience him.

One of my greatest honors and privileges as a grandmother is to pray for my grandchildren. I did not do this for my children, and I regret it deeply. What a blessing to be able to do so for my grandchildren. I am learning the depth and breadth of this call. I am grateful that these prayers can make a difference in their lives for eternity.

I have a prayer mentor. Her name is Debbie, and she is an intercessor extraordinaire. Small and slender like Mother Teresa, she is tiny in body but giant in spirit. Her prayers for her children, and for my children and grandchildren, blow me away. Like Brother Lawrence, she prays all the time. She sees every situation as an opportunity she can lift up before the Father. Every burden is a chance to listen and learn. Through prayer, she has grown in faith, able to see life from God's perspective.

From my interactions with Debbie, I am learning to live in the moment. I am appreciating life day by day. I am looking at life through a new paradigm. I am challenged to be more in line with God's perspective. It's not easy to make a shift at my age, but I figure if I don't do it now, I may miss my opportunity.

Life is full of these moments of revelation. What a motivation for me as a grandmother to keep my eyes open to experience and see their transforming power! Living in these moments is transformation at its best.

If I keep my eyes on God, "one day at a time" becomes a living, working reality in my life. Day by day, one step at a time—I am learning indeed.

SIX

CELEBRATE EVERY WRINKLE

Lord, you have been our dwelling place throughout all
generations. Before the mountains were born or you
brought forth the earth and the world, from everlasting
to everlasting you are God.

—Psalm 90:1-2

One of my favorite cinematic scenes is in the movie *Steel
Magnolias*. Truvy Jones (played by Dolly Parton) is standing on the porch of her beauty salon talking with young
Annette (played by Daryl Hannah). "Honey," Truvy says,
"time is marching on—and it is marching all over my face."

No words were truer than this. Time is marching on, and
not only is it marching over my face, but it has taken over
my whole body. As I recognize this phenomenon of aging, I
remind myself that I've earned every wrinkle. Every year their

numbers increase. We've been together so long now that we are becoming good friends.

I've always wondered if wrinkles could talk, what they might say. Perhaps the wrinkle on my forehead reflects the many hours I waited up for my children when they missed their curfews. Maybe the wrinkles around my mouth tell the story of my impatience and lack of trust in God, or those around my eyes indicate my mistakes and lost opportunities.

But there is another way to look at these characteristic indentations. Maybe the wrinkles on my forehead reflect how much time I spend thinking about those I love, studying the world around me and finding it good. The wrinkles around my mouth might come from the many times I have stood in awe at a beautiful sunset in the mountains, or marveled as a flower begins to open up in the garden. I like to think they imitate my smile as I offer thanks to God for his magnificent creation.

Perhaps the wrinkles around my eyes are laugh lines, memory boards that hold the experiences in life I have enjoyed and participated in the most. Perhaps the wrinkles on my face are a sign of life lived, of wisdom developed, trust earned.

Our culture is notorious for avoiding the aging process. We all know the commercials and gimmicks that promise to make us younger, firmer, trimmer, thinner, and the creams that promise to make us less wrinkled, more youthful, and more vigorous. Why can't we have rest? Is it not our time to celebrate? God created the world in six days, and even he rested.

I say yes—it is time. Call out the bands. Bring out the champagne. Put on your party shoes. Let's celebrate! We've earned it. Life is good, and I'm a grandmother four times over.

I am a member of a dance group, the Windsor Dance Club. We meet once a year to dance. From fifty to sixty-five years young, the members gather to dance till we drop. The only requirement is to love to dance. And we do dance.

As a safeguard, we control our membership by coordinating the minimum age requirement with our Social Security availability. The bad news is that our partying hours also reflect this approaching Medicare benefit. What used to be a blowout from 9 p.m. to 2 a.m. has now become a party from 7 p.m. to midnight. My fear is that we are moving toward the *Jerry Seinfeld* syndrome, with dinner at four thirty and dancing till seven.

Yes, it's time to celebrate being who God created us to be. Surely God knew what he was doing. Most definitely he had a plan for women after menopause. In his wisdom, he provided a phase of life when women are no longer able to create life. He moved us from child bearers to child encouragers, from life giving to life sustaining. This is a window of time in which we can be who we truly are.

Perhaps even silver hair has a purpose. I know it's beyond our ability to see or understand, but I am sure God's intentions were good. One purpose might be not to make us look older but to make us look softer, to bring out our eyes. Who can guess the mind of God?

A few years ago, I had the opportunity to test my hair theory in the most intimate of circumstances. I facilitated a breast cancer survivor group at a local hospital. Most of the women there were taking chemo and had lost their hair. All were wearing wigs. As their hair grew out and their spirits grew strong, many revealed themselves by removing their wigs. As each one unmasked herself, I was amazed by their individual uniqueness and perfect beauty. It was then and there that I vowed to unmask my own self—no matter the cost. Not dyeing my hair anymore was one way to do that.

God makes no mistakes. But, then, that's as it should be.

Time is indeed marching on, but perhaps it is not just marching over our faces. Maybe, just maybe, it is marching over our hearts, minds, and spirits. Instead of lamenting its progression, perhaps we need to celebrate and flex with its call.

Now that is something to celebrate!

PART 2

GRAND NEWS

SEVEN

NINE MONTHS AND COUNTING

"For I know the plans I have for you," declares the
LORD, "plans to prosper you and not to harm you, plans
to give you hope and a future."
—Jeremiah 29:11

M om, hi," says Lee on an unexpected Wednesday afternoon phone call. "What are you doing?" I can hear it in
his voice. I know. Somehow moms always know the signs of
important moments. They are pregnant, but I wait for him to
tell me the news.

"Are you sitting down? I have great news." I wait with
baited breath.

"We think Holly is pregnant." The celebration begins in
my head. I see fireworks. I hear drum rolls and music. I experience thunderous applause. The mountains have moved. It
has finally happened. The clock begins ticking.

I now have nine months to complete my preparation and training to be a grandmother.

I begin to listen with interest to friends who are already grandmothers. I am the world's worst shopper, but I start to browse baby stores, searching for updated baby equipment. I listen to the terminology of young moms and try to keep up. I better hurry if I am going to be ready for "B" day!

"Now don't become a loose cannon," Jim tells me, but I pay no attention. I'm going all out for this one.

Holly begins to plan the nursery. I have to be careful. Mothers-in-law are supposed to wear beige and keep their mouths shut. But I don't like beige, and I want my first grandchild to have the best. We shop together, and I buy a glider for the baby's room. Jim is not happy. I tell him, "Things are different now. I want my grandchild to have all the things my babies never had." We learn it is a boy. Now here is a place I can shine, for I am a two-time winner with boys.

I remember when Lee was born. We lived in an eighty-five-dollar-a-month walk-up in Galveston, Texas. My mom had shipped down my "kiddy coop" from WWII. It was old and looked like a cage, but we were glad to have it. Instead of a changing table, she helped me paint an old chest, and we sewed a plastic cushion with green flowers to lay the baby on. To complete the ensemble, we dyed an old rug olive green at the Laundromat. My kids never had a stroller, a jogger, or a glider. They were rocked to sleep in an unfinished Bentwood rocker. Not very comfortable but, hey, it did the trick. I always dreamed of more. Now was my chance.

I don't remember any prenatal preparation for my sons. No sonogram, amniocentesis, or Baby Bach. We just got pregnant, saw the doctor once a month, and then had the baby. Not so with this generation. Holly read everything in sight and worked until the day before she went into labor. What stamina! I remember the last days of my pregnancies hardly being able to get out of a chair, yet she was exercising till the last day.

"B" day arrives. Being induced is a miracle of science, like making a nail appointment, quite convenient for those who must travel a long distance for the birth. Some of my friends even keep open airline tickets and bags packed, prepared to leave at the first phone call. The way we are behaving, one would think we were the ones having the babies.

We drive to Austin the night before so we won't miss a moment. We take them out to dinner. Holly is calm, but I am on pins and needles, much more nervous than when I had my babies. They seem like children. Was I this young?

They begin to induce. A complication arises, and the doctor explains that the epidural is too risky. They have some decisions to make. They are scared.

Lee turns to Jim for advice. "Dad, what do we do?"

I'll never forget that moment. It stands out as a God-ordained moment in time. Jim slowly turns to Lee and says, "Son, this is your decision. We are going to step out of the room now while you and Holly discuss it. I know you will make the right decision."

How wise. What restraint. What good judgment. In that moment, Jim passes the torch of manhood to Lee.

Jim and I tremble with fear as we remove ourselves to the hall. We hold hands and pray.

The door remains closed for about five minutes. When it opens, a miracle has occurred. In the blink of an eye, these two children have become adults; they have become one. Before my very eyes, my son has become a man. What an awesome moment.

"We are going to have a baby," Lee says.

The nurse coaches him. He coaches Holly and together they bring a miracle into the world—a redheaded, eight-pound, nineteen-and-a-half-inch bundle of joy. The look on Lee's face when he opens the door to introduce his son to the family is forever etched in my memory.

It took nine months to make a baby. It took an instant to make a man. It took a lifetime to make a grandfather.

Nine months and counting—a grandmother is born!

EIGHT

I'M GOING TO BE A WHAT?

I will cause Your name to be remembered
in all generations.
—Psalm 45:17 NASB

Upon hearing the news that they are about to become grand-mothers, many women are shocked and taken aback. The news that they are no longer the "in" generation, but rather moving toward the title of senior and Medicare recipient, is more than some can bear.

Not me. I couldn't wait to be a grandmother. Rather than asking, "I'm going to be a what?" my question to my children was, "When am I going to be a grandmother?" Having grand-kids couldn't come fast enough for me.

Rather than picturing an old woman in a rocking chair, knit-ting and watching life as it passes by, I see the title as a promo-tion—a place of great opportunity, a professor with tenure, a retired CEO, a woman of great worth. I see every wrinkle, every gray hair as a badge of honor, a title well won. I view them as numerous threads weaving together to form a picture of life that can be handed down to another generation.

I loved being a mother. It was my life's work. When my children grew up and left home, I felt my chosen work on earth was over, complete, finis, kaput. There was so much I wish I had said, wish I had done—wish I could have done differently. I wish there had been more time. It all went by so fast.

As I shared this sentiment at my church circle, a sweet, dear, and very wise lady said to me, "Honey, don't fret. That's what I used to think. But then I realized that is why God made grandchildren. You get to do it all again, but better." And that's how I feel about being a grandmother.

Now don't get me wrong. There is a definite line between parenting and grandparenting. I will never be a parent again, nor do I want to. My life is full today. Never have I been more active. Never have I had more interests or been more involved in trying new things: hiking, organic gardening, learning Spanish and French, traveling, specialty cooking, volunteering, dancing, and bridge—the list goes on and on.

As a grandmother, I get to experience the best parts of parenting without the hassle. I get to love, listen, help, laugh, cry, rock, hold, sing, share, act silly, and make a mess—all in the name of grandparenting.

When my grandson Jack was about a year and a half, Jim and I took him out to dinner. It was late. He had had a big day, and it was his bedtime. As children are wont to do, he became fussy. Jim's response: "Well, we need to teach him to have manners and stay put until we are finished." My response: "No, we've been there, done that. It's not my job to discipline him. My job is to be present, attentive, hear him, and love him. Let his parents teach him manners. We're going home."

Now is that freedom or what?

Being a grandmother was not a shock to me. I have looked forward to it with great anticipation. I have so much to give and share, so much love to pass around. I am not encumbered or overwhelmed with the hassles of life. I am learning the art of being present in the moment. And that is the gift I leave my grandchildren—being present with them in all things.

I'm going to be a *what*? I'm going to be a grandmother. You bet I am.

NINE

WHAT'S IN A NAME?

You will be called by a new name
that the mouth of the LORD will bestow.
—Isaiah 62:2

What's in a name? Everything. A name tells who we are, what we believe, what we hope to be. In ancient times, a baby's name reflected a characteristic or a fact of life. *Moses*— drawn out of the water. *Jacob*—deceiver. *Matthew*—called of God. Today, we name our children after our forefathers or our favorite people. Someone whom we hope the child will emulate.

But no one has ever chosen his own name. Names are picked for us—until now. The day I found out I was going to become a grandmother, I began to think about my name. What would my grandchildren call me? It had to be unique. It had to be me. It had to be special. What should I be called?

I went through the usual choices: Grandmother, Nana, Mimi, Gammy—none of them seemed to fit. My own grandparents had such unique names: Shakey, Poppy, Gangy, Maman, Cecca, Buppy. I wanted something that was as special as these names, but how to choose one?

My husband had no problem. He knew immediately that he would be called Big Dad. And that was that. But for me, as the baby grew in utero, so did my anxiety. My daughter-in-law began to ask me what I wanted to be called. In our family we have an aunt we call Auntie Mar, after Auntie Mame in the movies. She thought I should be called Granny Mar. That was too much of a mouthful for me.

I began to research names. I asked my friends how they got their grandmother names. Gloria chose Gigi because of the G in her name and the G in grandmother. Lenda chose G because of the G in grandmother. D'Ann chose DD because it had a nice ring and because many of us called her that as a term of endearment. Bev became Dearie; she's not sure why. Courtney became CiCi because of her initials. Judie became Sweetie and Suzan, Mum Mum, named by their children. Carole chose Mumsie because it was the winner in her grandmother-naming contest.

What was I to do? As time moved on, I found I became adept at helping others come up with creative names: Anna

Jean became Nanny Jean, and Nelda became Nana. But I was stuck for want of a name.

Then one day I was flipping through the channels, and *Little Women* was on TV. There it was: Marme. It struck me like a bolt of lightning. Perfect. It sounded sort of like Marty, was catchy like Auntie Mar, and yet had a wonderful story and ideal behind it. Marme I would be.

I announced the good news to my family and friends, and they began to use the name when appropriate. I signed my cards and notes to my children this way and gave early baby gifts using my signature name.

Then the baby came. What a joy. For three months I was Marme, happy as a clam. Then one day my son said, "Mom, Holly and I have been talking. We don't think you are a Marme." What, not a Marme? How can this be?

Being the people-pleaser that I am, I asked what they thought I should be called. They didn't know, but thought I should try another name. So for a week I was Nana. Never seemed to fit but, hey, I'm a good sport. Thank goodness that after a few days Lee recanted and said he thought we'd made a mistake. Nana I was not. Could we go back to Marme?

What's in a name? Everything. And I got to choose mine. Is God good or what?

TEN

ON YOUR MARK, GET SET, GO!

For you created my inmost being;
you knit me together in my mother's womb.
I praise you because I am fearfully and wonderfully made.
—Psalm 139:13–14

D arin and Blythe are having their first baby. It is grandchild number four for us, and we find ourselves in the process of getting ready for our newest arrival.

The birthing process is an amazing thing. From conception to delivery, a miracle unfolds before our eyes. Even after three grandchildren, I never cease to marvel at the miracle of it all.

This one is a boy. Darin and Blythe are excited. My husband and I are excited too. I rejoice at my sons having their own sons just two years apart. I begin to plan campouts and hunting and skiing trips for them. What fun they will have!

This experience is different for us. While my other grand-children live four hours away in Austin, Darin and Blythe live in town about a mile from our house, so we are blessed to see their progress on a daily basis. We help them paint the baby's bedroom. One wall is dark brown, one tan, one light blue, and one turquoise. What can this possibly be? I am perplexed and cannot imagine how this is going to look. We are dutiful, however, and don't question. We finish our assignment and go home.

A few days later we get the phone call. "It is finished. Come and see."

An amazing transition has occurred. What looked like dis-connected dots and disjointed colors have been tied together into a perfect whole. The fabric and hand-painted stripes on the wall complete the project. It is perfect. It is them.

I am reminded that this painting process is not unlike the development of the embryo, cells and chromosomes com-ing together to make a perfect whole. A tiny person is being knit inside the womb, a perfect combination of a mother and father. Will he have her eyes, his hair?

Blythe has joined an Internet baby news service. Each week she sends me an update on the progress of the baby. This week the baby is opening and closing his eyes. Last week he began to develop fat in his skin. He hiccups, burps, and responds to food and sounds. He is real, unique, his own little person. They play music for him. They know what food he likes and dislikes. He is, indeed, a miracle, fearfully and wonderfully made.

They name him, but we will not learn his name until he is born. They call him by name when they talk to him. Darin sings to him in utero. He knows his father's touch. He becomes still and quiet when Darin touches him. Publicly we call him DuBob. I'm not sure how that started but everyone is doing it. I wonder if we will be able to change his name when he is born.

I think about my other three grandchildren. How amazing they are—a redhead, a strawberry blonde, and a towhead, all from the same parents. Unique and special, they are cells and chromosomes that have come together into perfect combinations of their parents.

We are in month seven now. The time goes slowly, yet it seems to fly by. I remember when I was pregnant. I can't remember a day when I didn't feel like a beached whale, large and cumbersome, awkward and clumsy. I was so large I could balance a butter dish on my stomach. I would spend hours on the sofa watching each little movement, marveling when a hand or foot pushed my abdomen. I remember propping my pillow behind me at restaurants to keep me comfortable.

My daughters-in-law don't seem to have these problems. They exercise and work until the due date. They look beautiful. Blythe's skin glows. She is filled with light and anticipation. She is counting the days.

They are getting set. They are planning natural childbirth. They are taking birthing classes. They have a doula who coaches them. They are at the starting line.

Nine months and counting—we are getting close! I can't wait. I count the days till we will meet him. I can't wait to count his fingers and toes. I count the years that have flown by since his father was conceived. I count my blessings with such great sons and amazing daughters-in-law. I count the years I have lived with their father. I count the memories we share.

Nine is the magic number. The baby is almost here. I wonder if my son and his wife will ever know how many nights we have stayed awake praying for this baby, praying for them. I wonder if they know the anticipation we have, the joy they bring. I wonder if they know how much we care.

It doesn't matter. To share their joy is enough.

On your mark, get set, go! Bring it on. I am ready.

ELEVEN

SHINE ON, SHINE ON HARVEST MOON

Arise, shine, for your light has come,
and the glory of the LORD rises upon you.
—Isaiah 60:1

It is a beautiful night. A full moon waits to cry out the news, preparing the way for new life. The harvest moon—bright, orange, and surrounded by clouds—stands guard as it awaits the birth of Baby Norman number four.

According to the encyclopedia, a *harvest moon* is the name given to the full moon that occurs nearest the autumnal equinox of the sun. It shines with such brightness that farmers in northern Europe and Canada can work until late in the night to take in the full harvest.

What a perfect metaphor for the birth of my fourth grandchild. Blythe and Darin are determined to bring this child into the world naturally. As they labor into the night, they bring in their harvest, their firstborn son. At 11:23 p.m., an eight-pound-three-ounce, nineteen-and-a-half-inch miracle is born.

I am reminded of a trip Jim and I recently took to Germany. In every church and cathedral, large or small, there were vegetables. Pumpkins, squash, cucumbers, and peppers spilled from the altar onto the surrounding floor—a plethora of colors, shapes, and sizes. I asked a passerby what this meant, and he explained the German custom of bringing in the first fruits, the biggest and best of the harvest, to the church as thank offerings for the bountiful harvest. This custom is probably the forerunner to our Thanksgiving. On this night, I couldn't help but think of our own Thanksgiving table—a cornucopia of color and texture. This little one represents for us this cornucopia of thanksgiving, the bounty of our blessing.

Serendipity surrounds his birth. Labor begins on a Sunday morning as Darin and Blythe visit the Japanese Gardens, the place where one year and one week ago to the day, they exchanged their wedding vows. I pondered the odds of such an occurrence.

After twelve hours, the baby finally arrives, and Darin makes the announcement. His name is Strother. They love the name. This is not a household word to us, but as Darin points out, with names like Darin and Blythe, what did we expect? I later do a Google search and am comforted to know there are seventy-nine pages of Strothers. It seems it is not as uncommon as first thought. Who knows? Maybe someday someone will Google *Strother*, and our Strother will be highlighted on page eighty. Even now there are signs of such a possibility. So far, an estimated four hundred visitors have logged on to Blythe's blog since his birth. Who knows how many "Strother watchers" there will be in twenty years?

I mark the differences in the birthing process since 1999. I am most unsettled by the increased security between this birth and Jack's. Jim and I are given hot-pink wristbands that identify us as visitors, and we have to sign a register in the waiting room. Both parents are given wrist bracelets to wear at all times. Their bands correspond with the baby's ankle bracelet. If they move more than twenty-five feet from him, an alarm alerts the nurse's station. Blythe cannot even walk down the hall alone. Her baby must be pushed in the bassinet beside her or sent to the nursery. There are no metal detectors yet, but I wonder how long it will be before they are needed. I am grieved that my grandchild will grow up in such a world.

I concentrate on the positive advances of our culture. Studies tell us that babies are aware of sounds, light, music, and voices in utero, and I believe it. When Strother is four days old, I stop by for a quick visit. Blythe pulls me into the kitchen to show me a video she has taken the day before.

Darin sits in the chair strumming his guitar as the baby is swaddled in his bouncy chair on the floor. Mesmerized by the music, his eyes never leave his father's face as he listens to *"La Tête Dans Les Nuages,"* the song Darin has written especially for him. In French it means "Head in the Clouds," and it has been sung to him many times in utero.

If I hadn't seen it with my own eyes, I would not have believed what happened next. As the last note is sung, Strother's eyes close as he falls asleep. His movements are timed with the music, perfectly choreographed, as if he knows the song is ending. I can't help but wonder if he has not heard this song before, perhaps lulled to sleep in a different time and a different place.

As my role of being a grandmother continues to grow, I am aware of how much I still have to learn. I can't wait to discover Strother and what he will become. Just as the German houses were individualized by paintings on the buildings, so, too, will Strother be individualized as he becomes his own designer, artist, and defining factor. As he reveals himself on a blank canvas, I will begin to see the picture of who he is.

In Italian, *birth* means coming into the light. A scene in the movie *Under the Tuscan Sun* with Diane Lane best describes this miracle of new life. Surrounded by the enchanting colors of Tuscany, Diane holds her friend's newborn baby close and walks to the window. She throws open the shutters and faces the rising sun. "Welcome to the light," she says, as the new day dawns.

This is how I feel about Strother's birth. In my mind's eye, I hold this precious life close, walk to the window, throw open the shutters, lift him to the light, and whisper, "Welcome to the light, my precious grandchild." I give thanks for the miracle of his birth.

Shine on, shine on harvest moon—the harvest has come.

TWELVE

CHANGING GRANDMOTHER IMAGES

The LORD will guide you always;
he will satisfy your needs in a sun-scorched land
and will strengthen your frame.
You will be like a well-watered garden,
like a spring whose waters never fail.
—Isaiah 58:11

When I was young, I never visualized myself as a grand-mother.

In my mind's eye, I still see myself as a nineteen-year-old girl, happy and feisty, raring to go. I loved my grandmother, but back when I was nineteen, she looked to me a bit old, slow, saggy, and out of step. She wore black high-tops and smelled of talcum powder and lilac. She played solitaire and canasta and told lots of stories. She was great fun, but definitely not someone I wanted to be.

I tolerated the grandmothers of my friends. Nona's Ma-Maw took us on the train to Galveston. Carol's Biggie lived at the lake. Lucy's Grandmother Margaret sat in a chair and refused to go out. Back then, grandmothers were too much of a stretch for me.

The first time I realized I was a grandmother, I was walking toward a glass door, reaching for the handle. I saw a gray-haired woman approaching from the other side. I remember thinking, *Oh my, what is my mother doing here?*

You guessed it. Walking toward me were my mother's gait, mannerisms, and hair, but it was not my mother. It was me.

In that moment, I made a paradigm shift. I began the process of upgrading my perception of grandmothers and determined that I would be a new-generation grandmother. I vowed that I would never go gray—despite my hair color!

In that instant, my image of grandmothers was transformed. Now, rather than old, I see mature. Rather than saggy, I see soft. I wear flip-flops instead of high-tops and smell of Chanel N°5. My hair is silver, not gray, and I am not slow and out of step, but thoughtful and consistent.

I began to notice grandmothers in earnest. One year, as I was facilitating a continuing education course at Texas Christian University, titled Grandmother Connections, I took a closer look at the women who came to the class. They were not old, nor did they act old. They were accomplished, active, self-confident, classy, and had a contagious joy. They played the piano, picked up their grandchildren from school, traveled around the world, were at the top of their careers, dressed hip, attended recitals and soccer games, laughed a lot, and looked great. Sylvia teaches piano lessons. Sue has ten grandchildren, and Joan just returned from the maiden voyage of the *Queen Mary II*. Jean has tenure as a college professor. As they shared their stories, I was so impressed with them. They were filled with celebration, joy, and challenge. But none of these women were discouraged, hopeless, or helpless. None seemed old or gray to me.

So what is old? I began to wonder. Webster's defines *old* as "having lived or existed for a long time." That definition certainly fits my outside, but it falls far short of describing my inside. Inside of old is a lifetime of wisdom, a plethora of memories, an arbor of life lessons.

A few years ago in my practice as a therapist, I had a client named Jane. I adored Jane. She was eighty-five, and her story was amazing. She had endured the Great Depression, World War II, infertility, adoption of two children (one a special-needs child), and was widowed at an early age, yet she was feisty and full of vim and vigor. I asked her the secret of her attitude, and she confided, "You need to have a sense of humor and a belief in God. If you can laugh at yourself, then nothing can daunt you." She followed this axiom to the end, continuing her sense of humor and faith even on her deathbed. Jane taught me about grandmother images.

I don't know if grandmothers have changed or if my perception of grandmothers has changed. I don't know if my grandchildren see me as old or as well-worn but still kicking. I hope that they see the "me" that God sees, the child inside whom he created.

Of course, it really doesn't matter what they see. Grandmothers are what they are: fountains of love and joy, living water poured out upon young lives. Image or no image, we have the opportunity to breathe life.

And that is no image—that is reality.

PART 3

GRAND OPPORTUNITIES

THIRTEEN

BUT WE ALWAYS DO IT LIKE THAT

"For my thoughts are not your thoughts, neither are
your ways my ways," declares the LORD.
—Isaiah 55:8

Although Kenny Rogers is not a philosopher, some of the songs he performs have great wisdom. One of my favorites is "The Gambler," which uses a game of cards as a metaphor for life. Singing of discernment and choices, the message is universal. Whether we have a pair or a full house, our job is to learn to live with the cards we are dealt.

Our world would do well to emulate Kenny Rogers's wisdom. As grandmothers, we have collected many cards. Our hands are more than full. If we check closely, surely there are some winners in there somewhere. Since it is too late to reshuffle the deck, we must somehow find a way to discard the unused cards and deal with what we have. In the words of the song, we have to know what to keep, when to keep it, and when to let go:

> You've got to know when to hold 'em,
> Know when to fold 'em,
> Know when to walk away,
> Know when to run.
> You never count your money,
> When you're sittin' at the table,
> There'll be time enough for countin',
> When the dealin's done.

Family traditions are a lot like this song.

Most families have traditions. The importance of these family traditions cannot be underestimated. The problem is that some family traditions are outdated and need to be eliminated while other traditions are inflexible and set in stone. Somehow we have to find a way to break down the walls and institute new traditions.

When I was a practicing therapist, I often saw much conflict when two families are joined together in holy matrimony. As husband and wife unite two different families, sometimes their families' traditions come into direct conflict with one another. When this happens, someone has to change.

The good news is that traditions don't have to be inflexible. They can change or be created at any time, in any place, for any purpose. They can be altered, edited, or modified at will. There are no rules. The sky is the limit.

Grandchildren are great at creating traditions. They have no preconceived ideas of what their family traditions should be. The adults are the problem. Grandchildren are open to new ideas. This is good news for grandmothers. All we need to do is be flexible. How easy is that?

Since most traditions revolve around holidays, it is important to be creative. One of the favorite traditions at my house is decorating Christmas cookies. It has become a huge affair with contests and prizes, enduring well past college years into adulthood.

Since my children are tied to their office schedules, fitting this activity into the limited time their families are able to visit us for Christmas is a huge challenge. The process is exhausting. Mainly it is a lot of work for me. Balancing this with meals and opening presents was causing chaos in my family and ill will with the in-laws. One day I realized I needed a new plan.

A Tri Delt fund-raiser, Cookies and Castle, quickly became my plan B. Situated in a banquet hall with tables overflowing with candy, it is a child's playground. Surrounded by ginger snaps, wheat Chex, ice cream cones, coconut, licorice, and

M&Ms, it is an eat-till-you-drop affair—a perfect grandmother opportunity. And the best part: since it is in early December, there is less competition for time.

Thus, I have started a new tradition. The grandchildren come for an overnight in early December. This is easy to schedule, is much less hassle for me, and requires no cleanup. The grandkids love it and look forward for months to their opportunity to decorate gingerbread houses.

A tradition is born.

For in-town grandkids, traditions are much easier and more flexible. My cousin George has "Christmas with Grandma." No one knows exactly what goes on at this affair because parents are not included. We do know that the activity involves food, a play, costumes, and singing. My cousins tell me it is their favorite Christmas activity.

Some traditions can be expensive, but they are well worth the money. My friend Courtney joins six mothers, daughters, and grandmothers to attend the *Nutcracker* each December. Dressed in their Sunday best, they follow the performance with a tea party—fun for young and old alike.

The best traditions cost no money at all. My grandson James enjoys driving around looking at Christmas lights. He doesn't care how many or how extravagant they are. He just loves being there. I suspect that singing is really his main motivation, since he requests "Jingle Bells" over and over, but somehow the moving car creates the perfect ambiance. I wouldn't miss this special time with him for the world. I even make a special trip to Austin to do it.

Grandmothers are the best at traditions, for they know the secret. It doesn't matter what kind of tradition one has; what is important is that the child knows the steps.

If we are smart, as grandmothers we will take a hard look at the hand we have been dealt in this life. After all, there is probably an ace in there somewhere!

Every gambler knows, the secret to survivin',
Is knowin' what to throw away, knowin' what to keep.
Cause every hand's a winner, and every hand's a loser . . .

Pulling out the ace at the proper time makes us all winners. No need to gamble at all.

FOURTEEN

DEALING WITH RETIREMENT WHILE DRIVING TO MUSEUM SCHOOL

Teach us to number our days aright, that we may gain
a heart of wisdom.
—Psalm 90:12

When are you going to retire? That is the question of my generation. My answer—I will never retire. I will just continue to retread until I keel over.

This thought occurred to me while I was driving my grandchildren to museum school during a ten-day visit one summer. And then I knew: I had driven this road before. Many a summer I packed my own kids in the car, driving them to learn about the mysteries of the universe and the patterns of the night sky. How quickly the years have passed. Now I am driving that same road again, literally and figuratively. But this time there is a lot of wear and tear on my tires, and I have been bolstered and reworked from head to toe a number of times.

I remember my mother telling stories of World War II. That was the day of retread tires. For five years cars were driven as they were, or the tires were retread. No new tires were available. In fact in the second month of life, I was placed in a car with retread tires. It was April 1945, and my mother, grandmother, and aunt drove me, a six-week-old baby, to Maine, perched in a dog basket in the back of the Ford Sedan. We drove all the way on scary mountain passes and retread tires. We persevered and survived. In fact, that is when my grandmother got her grandmother name, Shakey. She was so scared driving through the mountains that my aunt nicknamed her after a Dick Tracy character in the funny papers. And Shakey we called her until the day she died.

There is a lesson to be learned about retread tires, for they are not all bad. They kept on working, served their purpose, and were useful until the end of the war. Everyone was grateful to have them, because they met a need. That sounds a lot like me: a grandmother dealing with retirement and museum school. Just call me Retread.

I'm not sure Jim and I even know what retirement really is. Jim dreams of retirement as fishing in Colorado, sailing around the Florida Keys, or building a ranching empire in West Texas.

Instead, we find ourselves saddling horses for grandkids, baiting hooks with worms, and wearing floaties in the swimming pool. Retread. I've done this before.

Statistics tell us that many seniors are coming out of retirement and starting new businesses. Others are creating job opportunities for supplemental income, such as marketing specialists, Internet salesmen, or Wal-Mart greeters. And they are doing a great job. Retreads again—recycling the past, transforming what is known and adapting it. As grandparents, we are really good at this.

There are even retreads in the Bible. I am reminded of Moses, who lived a life of luxury in the palace and was treated as Pharaoh's son. Then he was exiled from his country, forced to live in the desert at the age of forty. Over a period of years, he tended the flocks, lived a humble life as a shepherd, and experienced God in a profound way. As he grew in age and stature, he also gained in experience, influence, and wisdom. Later he returned to Egypt to meet a need, live in obedience to his God, fulfill his purpose, and deliver God's people from bondage. His life had been reworked, the wear and tear on his person molded and reshaped to God's specifications— a retread, reworked and recycled to be used for God's good purpose.

My friends and I are in the same recycle mode. Constantly

being overhauled and reworked, we find ourselves returning to the places of our youth. Hopefully, this time we have more wisdom and experience under our belts. A sign that reminds us of our place in the life cycle is on Wednesday mornings, when you see our vehicles lined up for coffee with car seats in the back. If we didn't have sags and wrinkles and experience written across our foreheads, you would think we were twenty-five again.

But I wouldn't change a thing. I love being a retread. Just pack me up and bring me in. Give me an overhaul every three months, and I'm ready to go back out on the road.

Retirement—who needs it? My vote goes for recycling, overhauls, and retreads.

FIFTEEN

WITHER THOU GOEST

Where you go I will go, and where you stay I will stay.
Your people will be my people and your God my God.
—Ruth 1:16

In-law or outlaw? That is the question. Every grandmother is one or the other. Which are you?

A study on families indicates that mothers are almost always in. That's a given, but the jury is still out on mothers-in-law. Yet we have more impact than we know on whether we are considered "in" or "out." The good news is that having relationships with our daughter-in-laws is not only possible but has great potential.

I am blessed with two wonderful daughters-in-law. If I had handpicked wives for my sons, I could not have done a better job than these two women. God outdid himself on this one. Each is a perfect complement and mate for my boy. Each brings her own gifts and talents to our family mix, rounding us out in a special way.

For centuries, many cultures placed great value on the wisdom that comes with age and respected their elders, especially the mother-in-law. Historically, it was the mother-in-law who mentored, taught, and guided the family. Not so today. The mother-in-law joke is, as best I can tell, a twentieth-century invention. Regardless of its origin, the wedding advice to wear beige and keep our mouths shut has a ring of truth to it. If we are in conflict with our daughters-in-law, it would serve us well to take deeper looks and discover the truths in our own lives that might be contributing factors to the controversy and to set things right.

The truth is that mothers have been around from birth to puberty. They have developed close relationships with their children. Mothers-in-law are latecomers. They are coming in at halftime. The game plan has changed, but often the team captains haven't realized it yet. It takes time to develop relationships, to create trust. The good news is that we mothers-in-law have a lot of time.

Often when engagements are announced, most of us expect our daughters-in-law to be instant Ruths. We are eager for them to abandon their homelands and join us in ours. No matter that they may be totally foreign cultures. I maintain that it takes many years to make a Ruth. But by the same token, it takes even more years to make a Naomi.

The fact is that I will always be a mother-in-law. Like it or not, that is the reality. The sooner I accept this, the better. Once the happy couple says *I do*, the equation changes. In my son's life, I am out and she is in. That is as it should be. The marriage ceremony tells us that a man is to leave his mother and father and cleave to his wife. They are now a family, and his first priority is his wife.

The good news is that I get to build a new relationship with my son; we have nowhere to go but up. With time on my side and patience in my corner, the tides will turn if I am willing. It took me a while to figure this out. I confess that at first I wasn't sure exactly where I fit. I questioned daily whether I would ever have a place in my son's life again.

I came face-to-face with this dilemma the month following the wedding. Holly and Lee moved to Austin for graduate school. We had planned our yearly vacation in Colorado between the honeymoon and the beginning of classes so they could join us. As it turned out, Holly got a job that began the week of our vacation. Lee was determined that he was coming to Colorado anyway. Holly was crushed, of course, that he wasn't planning to stay with her in Austin. Much to my dismay,

Jim advised him to stay home with his wife. In my heart of hearts, I knew this was wise counsel. But inside my heart was crying, *Oh, no. I have lost him forever! He will never come home for Christmas again!*

This was FEAR (future events appearing real), and, as one might suspect, these fears were unfounded. We have enjoyed more than ten years of not only Christmas celebrations with Lee and Holly but also many summers fishing on the Lake Fork of the Gunnison together.

The hardest part of being a mother-in-law has to do with the grandchildren. I give thanks to Holly in this area because she has been patient and loving with me, helping me to find my way. When my first grandchild was born, she wanted her mom to come to help first. Of course—all women want their moms. I wanted my mom. This is what we know; this is what we are comfortable with. This is not a time to take offense. This is not about us; it is about our role. Moms represent the known; mothers-in-law, the unknown. It is only through the test of time that this type of trust can be built. All mothers-in-law have got to come to terms with this fact. By the same token, the wife's mother needs to be sensitive to the situation, to the mother-in-law's position, and encourage her daughter to be inclusive and share.

Of course, we have a place. But like early marriage, relationships have to be built, and trust has to develop. The Naomi-Ruth relationship develops over many years. My friend Jean taught me a lesson in this type of relationship. Last summer she drove twice a week from Maine to Boston to support her daughter-in-law, an only child, as she tended to her dying mother. For twenty-four hour shifts, she sat at the bedside of her daughter-in-law's mother as a love offering to her daughter-in-law. Now that is the kind of Naomi I want to be.

My own Naomi-Ruth relationships are doing well. I am pleased with how Holly and I have built a good relationship over the years. She has gone above and beyond and is wonderful to include me. I respect and admire her and am in awe of her gifts and talents. I believe that she has come to appreciate me too. I am so grateful that we are walking this path of discovery together—one I cherish and give thanks for.

I know that as Blythe and Darin begin their family, I can also look forward to developing and growing with her. I can't wait to discover how to walk alongside her in whatever way she needs and in whatever way I can be of service. Already we have gotten off to a great start. I love how she loves my son, how much she nurtures and cares for him. I give thanks for how much she brings out the best and tender side of him. Yes, we have a great beginning.

Wither thou goest? I'm not quite a Naomi yet, but at least I am finding my way.

Thanks be to God.

SIXTEEN

DOCTOR, LAWYER, INDIAN CHIEF

For this cause we also, since the day we heard it, do
not cease to pray for you, and to desire that ye might
be filled with the knowledge of his will in all wisdom
and spiritual understanding.

—Colossians 1:9 KJV

Ask any group of children these days what they want to be when they grow up, and their answers will likely range anywhere from astronaut to zookeeper, with lots of layers in between. In these answers, children are expressing their personalities, experiences, and dreams.

When I was about six or seven years old, I remember staying with my great-grandmother Gangy while my parents went to Annapolis for a wedding. While I was there, I began writing my first novel. The main character was Tad. I have no idea what the plot was, but I know I wanted to create something for Tad. I also loved to make up songs. *Lollipop in the Windowsill* was my first big hit. As I look back, I see that my stories revealed a lot about me.

I don't remember sharing or talking about these things to anyone. Perhaps I did, perhaps not. But today at sixty, that is exactly what I am doing—writing and creating. Instead of novels, I write about life. Instead of songs, I write poetry. Why it took so long to recapture these dreams I will never know, but it is clear that childhood dreams have potential.

When our grandchildren tell us what they want to be when they grow up, we grandmothers can listen, encourage, educate, share, and help them explore these desires. My granddaughter Lily loves the color pink. She is almost obsessed with it. Everything she owns is pink, and when we make up stories, she always clothes the snakes or saddles in pink. I don't have a clue what this means. Maybe she has an eye for color. Perhaps she will be an artist or a fashion designer or a decorator. Perhaps I can encourage her interest by introducing her to the many shades of pink. An idea might be to get her a palette where we mix different colors of pink. A variation would be to collect scraps of pink for her to put on her cardboard doll, mixing and matching the pinks. Who knows what will come of this? The important thing for me is to be aware and attentive, to listen and follow up with my grandchildren's dreams.

Jack has always been fascinated by garbage trucks. Now his younger brother, James, sits on the curb and watches them too. Perhaps it's the noise; perhaps it's a boy thing. Either way, it is an opportunity. I bought them a book about garbage called *You Stink*. They love it. We spend hours poring over the pictures of the things people throw away. We discuss why. Was it really time to throw these things away? Who knows to what career this might lead? I do know they are gaining an appreciation for conservation, learning about stewardship and recycling. It may turn into a career, or it may not; but in the meantime, we are interacting on a most personal level.

The nursery rhyme "Doctor, Lawyer, Indian Chief" is a great reminder that we don't know what the future holds. We don't know in what directions our grandchildren will choose to walk. What we do know is that we are privileged to walk along the paths and share the journeys. Who knows, maybe someday one will say, "I became a famous wardrobe designer because my Marme cut out swatches of pink for me, and we mixed and matched outfits."

Now wouldn't that be the nuts?

SEVENTEEN

LOVE IS THE ANSWER

And now these three remain: faith, hope and love.
But the greatest of these is love.
—1 Corinthians 13:13

Looking back at my early years as a mother, I am reminded of how little I knew and how much I learned in a short span of time. Sometimes it all seems a blur.

I do remember being very busy. There were always meals to cook, diapers to wash (this was before disposable diapers, of course), rooms to clean, a carpool to run. It seems that I was permanently bent over in a "toy retrieval" mode. I remember being the queen of multitasking, something long since forgotten. I also remember a lot of laughter, a lot of crying, and many nights without sleep. But all in all, it was the best of times.

As I look back and reflect, I confess that I have many regrets.

My son, Lee, asked me once, if I could do it over again, what would I do differently?

I thought about it a moment and then said, "I think I would have held you more, rocked you more, sung more songs. I would have worried less about the house and just enjoyed each moment to its fullest. I would have taken more pictures, baked more cookies, and built more sandcastles." Then I added, "If I could do it over again, I would do exactly what I am doing now. There is so much love to give and so little time."

I could see him taking it all in. I see signs that he did. Lee is a great father—he's patient, creative, and fun, somehow finding quality time for each of his three children. I am so grateful and proud of him, for I know that at his age, I didn't have a clue.

But now I do know, and that's the best part of being a grandmother. I get to do all of these things and more. The older I get, the more I realize that things don't matter; people do. What is important is family, relationships, and God. When push comes to shove, that's all we really have.

I have a friend, George, who lives in Gulfport, Mississippi. Last year, Hurricane Katrina destroyed his family home of eighty-plus years. All of his memories and material belongings were blown away in one night. I asked him how he was handling the situation. I was stunned at his response: "You know, the Lord giveth and the Lord taketh away. Blessed be the name of the Lord! I have my life, and all of my family is safe. I am a rich man indeed. I will rebuild."

His attitude was certainly a life lesson for me, and one that I hope to incorporate into my own life.

I can't help but reflect on how I would react if a similar situation happened to me. What would be my attitude? What if I had to rebuild my home from scratch? What would that look like?

What came to me was an image of a house, standing tall and straight on top of a hill. I could only see the foundation and the framework, but I could tell it was a sturdy house and a strong foundation. Around the perimeter of the house was a tilled garden with three large sunflowers in bloom. Their vibrant yellow petals greeted the morning sun as they danced to the tune of a gentle breeze.

At once I knew the meaning of the image. This house was my spiritual house. Clearly, the house and the surrounding garden and contents represented the important things in my life. I knew I needed to take inventory of my spiritual condition to determine what I might need to remodel or rebuild.

First, I checked my foundation. Without a strong foundation, the house will not stand. It is the most important part of my house. I know that the foundation must be built on faith, so how is my faith?

Faith, then, is the first flower. After years of struggle and searching, heartache and tears, I have found that faith. Once my house was built on shifting sand, but today, the foundation is strong and firm. It is built on a rock. Any storms that come might threaten to blow the house down, but my house is not dependent on the things of this world. Although in my picture the house is just a frame, that's not what is important. The frame can be decorated or walled in. Better still, it can be left open to the cool breeze flowing around and through it. What is important is the foundation—the faith.

Second, my house must be surrounded by hope. Just as the garden surrounds the house, so, too, hope surrounds me. In my heart I carry the hope of new growth, of springtime blossoms, of eternity. Hope, then, is the second flower. Though the soil is only tilled and not yet in full bloom, I am excited about the future—what is growing, what is yet to come.

Last but not least, the third and most precious flower of all is love. My house must be built on love. Love is the answer. Love is the hope of all things. The apostle Paul says that without love we are as a resounding gong or a clanging cymbal (1 Cor. 13:1). Love is the hope of the world. It is the only hope that we have as a civilization.

As I reflect back to my answer to Lee's question, I'm not sure I would do differently. But I think I would do sooner. I would come to faith earlier. I would be more hopeful, looking at life with an eternal perspective. But most of all, I would open myself up to love, to giving and receiving, to being a receptacle that holds and dispenses love without judgment or prejudice.

Then when the storms come and the lightning flashes, when the sand shifts and the house falls, I will be ready. Standing on a firm foundation, I will be surrounded by the gentle arms of a loving God.

The answer to the question of what my house would look like if I had to rebuild, what my attitude might be, is love.

I hope that, like George, I would turn to God who is love. He is the answer.

EIGHTEEN

EVERY GRANDCHILD A WINNER

> But those who hope in the Lord will renew their strength.
> They will soar on wings like eagles; they will run and not
> grow weary, they will walk and not be faint.
> —Isaiah 40:31

Every grandchild is special, a unique gift of love sent by God to learn and grow, to give and receive life, to bless families with his or her uniqueness.

Lately I've been concerned about what I call the "baby supermarket" mentality. I read of people who, through the advances of modern science, are able to determine the gender or eye color of their unborn child. Instead of conception being a God-given gift, we are turning children into a commodity to be chosen and selected, discarded or changed. We are not satisfied with less than perfect. I fear by doing so we are losing the excitement of the journey. We are missing out on God's plan and purpose, and that grieves me greatly.

Today there are ways to test an unborn child's genetic makeup. Some of these tests are good, of course, but more often than not, many are cause for more stress and worry. When Holly was about three months pregnant with Jack, one of her blood tests came back positive. The doctors told her that there was a 95 percent chance that Jack had Down syndrome. We were all devastated, of course. We had to wait ten days for the amniocentesis. I called my prayer group for prayers. Jim and I tried to be supportive and encourage them the best way we knew how, but I confess that we were scared. Her amniocentesis showed that she had a false positive, and Jack did not have that syndrome. Yet I remember thinking about all those for whom the test does not show a false positive. How do they cope? What do their parents and grandparents think? What is it like for them?

I am honored and privileged to belong to a group called the First Grandmothers' Club. This is an idea inspired by my good friend, Lenda, who was so overwhelmed by the birth of her first grandchild and the love she felt that she wanted to do more. As she thought about all the things she wanted to do for her grandchildren, she began to ponder other children, those who had no advocate, no resource, no grandmother to help and guide them. Her passion was to find a way to impact the lives of the "least of these" (Matt. 25:40 KJV). Her desire was to share the love with them in whatever way she could.

Lenda took action and founded the First Grandmothers' Club, made up of first-time grandmothers. As the club grew, we began to seek out agencies that serve children with special needs. We educated ourselves on their situations and discussed ways we could help. We began donating to their well-being. We set up monthly meetings in order to broaden our perspective.

One of these programs was with two nationally recognized schools—one helps children with Down syndrome, and the other assists kids with learning difficulties. Both were started and initially funded by grandparents who had a special-needs grandchild. When they saw a need, they stepped in and took action. I was honored and privileged to be the First Grandmothers' Club board member in charge of this program. When I began, I knew very little about either.

In the course of the planning, I met Susan, a young mother who was one of the members on the panel. She has a Down syndrome child and a child with learning differences. Her testimony was nothing short of amazing. It was in her story that I got my answer to how people cope with a special-needs child. Susan's walk has not been easy, but the joy she exhibits when she talks of her children, the delight she receives from their successes, and the amazing love that pours out from her put me to shame.

Susan's wise perspective brought clarity to me that every child is, indeed, a winner. Her attitude and faith have made the difference. Her mother—the grandmother—has been the wind beneath her wings. She has been there every step of the way, helping and supporting, carrying and sustaining. Their faith is strong. Their lives are living examples of God's love and grace.

My eyes have, indeed, been opened. My paradigm has shifted. I see grandmothers in a new light. In my opinion, there is no better role for us than to see our grandchildren through the eyes of love as have Susan, her mom, and my friend, Lenda. No matter the circumstance, no matter the difficulty, we can be pillars of hope, beacons of strength to lift our children and grandchildren to new heights.

Are there lessons to be learned here? There sure are for me. Is every grandchild a winner? You bet he is . . . and more.

PART 4

GRAND CHALLENGES

NINETEEN

WHAT'S A FEW MILES IN THE SCHEME OF THINGS?

> May the LORD keep watch between you and me when
> we are away from each other.
> —Genesis 31:49

When I was little, my grandmother lived about four blocks away. I could ride my bike from my house to hers in about ten minutes. I loved to visit my grandma Shakey. We sat on the back porch in the evenings and caught lightning bugs in a jar. Some nights I would walk on the golf course with my grandfather and run through the sprinklers. My favorite pastime was playing with paper dolls from *McCall's* magazine. Shakey saved them for me weekly, so each visit was a new adventure.

Helen, my stepdad's mother, lived a few blocks further. We visited her too. She always served her special homemade cinnamon applesauce, and she hooked her own rag rugs. I used to sit and watch her braid the brightly colored lengths of fabric. In fact, in my first apartment, I hooked my own rug using her materials and tools.

Living near extended family and grandparents is a plus in life that cannot be measured. The constant contact, reinforcement, unconditional love, and mentoring from those older and wiser have the potential to broaden any child's world in unknown ways.

It was, therefore, a shock when Lee and Holly moved to Austin, where three of my grandchildren now reside. Not to be next door, not to be near on a daily basis, what is a grandmother to do?

Unfortunately, this scenario is not uncommon. With global travel and nanotechnology, many families find themselves in foreign lands, far from extended family and needed support. Many of my friends in Fort Worth have children now living in California, New York, and Boston. Some live even as far away as Costa Rica, Europe, and Japan. Being a long-distance grandmother is definitely a challenge, but many have risen to the occasion with creative ways to stay involved in their grandchildren's lives. I am learning from them how to bridge the distance and miles.

Judie reads books on tapes and sends them to her grandchildren in Atlanta, so they can hear her voice reading their favorite stories. Jean has started a book club with her grand-daughter. Every month she sends her a Barnes & Noble gift certificate, finds out the name of the book her granddaughter chooses, and then buys her own copy. They e-mail back and forth about the book, interacting and sharing their passion for reading. Another friend exchanges videos and digital pictures with her grandchildren in Israel on a daily basis. When my grandchildren were little, I pasted a picture of Jim and me on a small tape recorder. We taped short messages to them: "I love you! I miss you!" Lee says they played our voices over and over.

Some of my friends go above and beyond. Carole invites her out-of-town niece to her home in what they affectionately call Camp Cowtown, where the emphasis is play. My cousins George and Nancy invite their five grandchildren to Fredericksburg, Texas, for Camp Fred. My friend Carolyn takes her grandchildren to the beach each year. Spending a week together at the seashore is a great way to spend quality time. D'Ann and Bill rent a room in a hotel when they go to visit and have the grandchildren come there. They pop popcorn, watch movies, order room service, swim, and pretend to be on vacation.

As the kids have gotten older, we have encouraged them to call us whenever they want. Not long ago, Jack called at seven fifteen one morning, full of information about his new backpack, soccer game, and Lily's painted seashells. Our forty-five minute conversation may have run up the phone bill, but it was worth every penny.

There are many creative ways to stay involved with grandchildren, even from a distance. It's not the same as being there, but developing relationship and companionship is the name of the game. Even an in-town grandparent can take for granted the presence of a grandchild and not spend quality time. If a grandchild lives far away, we had best do our research, find out what that child likes to do, visit as often as possible, and set aside time to spend with each child, doing what they love to do. Soon traditions will be established and memories built.

There are many ways to stay connected, but traveling to them seems to be the norm. My in-laws used to claim that all they saw on the highway on Christmas morning were grandparents in cars piled high with gifts, traveling to see their children and grandchildren. I didn't believe them at the time, but now I'm beginning to think they were right on target.

Long-distance grandparenting is, indeed, a challenge. Rather than four blocks away, our grandchildren may live four states away. But to a creative grandmother, what's a few miles in the scheme of things?

TWENTY

SANDWICHING GRANDCHILDREN BETWEEN PARENTS AND CHILDREN

I am the bread of life. He who comes to me will never go
hungry, and he who believes in me will never be thirsty.

—John 6:35

When I was a child, my favorite sandwich was potato chip and mustard on white bread. My mother did not allow such abominations in the house, but for my grandmother and me, it was a great secret. Today I have graduated to cucumber and cream cheese on whole wheat pita, but I have never forgotten the taste of potato chips, mustard, and sliced bread. I often find myself tempted to return to those days of simpler tastes.

Today I am my own unique concoction, sandwiched between parents, children, and grandchildren. On a daily basis, I find myself pulled in multiple directions, torn by job responsibilities, family obligations, personal desires, leisure activities, and of course, grandchildren.

Such is the fate of my generation.

But there is good news. Grandmothers are up to the task. We are the best-kept secret since sliced bread.

I have finally accepted the fact that I am in process and am creating a living sandwich in action. Rather than being torn in the middle, I am a chef in culinary school, a Julia Child in the making. I have options.

This is how my sandwich works.

The outer part of me is the bread that holds everything together. This is the most important part, the God part, manna rained down on my life, exactly what I need for each day. My inner "fixin's" are made up of my parents, in-laws, and children. They are the meat of my life, the substance from which I came, the future to which I aspire. The good news is that I get to choose the type of bread I use to surround them—white or brown, stale or molded. I can disperse blessing or curse, depending on my inner thermometer.

I am privileged to serve those I love. As I search my pantry of history and life experience, I get to choose joy and thanksgiving or grumbling and murmuring.

Each day is a tightrope. The best way for me to handle this tightrope is to view my grandchildren as the flavor in my sandwich. No matter what type of bread I use, no matter what my meat and condiments are, my grandchildren are the spice that flavors me and gives my life that special aroma of fresh bread—sliced bread at its best.

It is true for all of us. No matter how down we get, no matter what life brings, it is God, the bread of life, and our grandchildren, the flavor in our sandwich, that give meaning and purpose to our lives. Grandchildren are as *salt*; they bring out the best in us. They are as *spice*; they keep us thinking and on our toes. They are as *marinade*; the longer we are with them, the better we become. And the best part is that we never know what each new day will bring, what will be used in our sandwich making.

Jim is an only child. Recently we moved his parents to our hometown so that we could better care for their needs. I confess that there was a moment when I wondered if this might be a huge barrier in my life. But the most marvelous surprise happened. Science teaches us that like species seek one another. And such has been the case with our family. I have found that when I have the grandchildren and the great-grandparents visiting at the same time, a wonderful connection occurs. The other day I looked out my window and saw my six-year-old grandson holding the hand of my ninety-year-old father-in-law, searching for pecans together. I just sat down and cried at the miracle of life—manna pouring down from the God of heaven.

By the same token, my eighty-two-year-old mother, who is extremely active and in better shape than I, adores spending time with my grandchildren. I find that I rely on her often when they are in town. She is game to do anything. Once she beat both Jack and me at golf. We accused her of showing off, but she just laughed and said it was "old-timer's" luck—you have to be over eighty to know the secret. She loves to babysit, and I love to listen to her as she reads a story to my grandchildren or plays a favorite game. I marvel at her patience as she taught Jack at age two how to distinguish between the T and J in an alphabet puzzle. She pointed out that the J is the one that looks like a fish hook. Now why didn't I think of that?

Creating a new sandwich is not so bad. My outer pieces, the God pieces, give me life, breath, and fill my life with spiritual food. The inner fixin's, the ones to whom I gave life, are the strength that holds my sandwich together. The grandchildren are the flavor that delights my palette on a daily basis. The condiments are the parts I get to bring out of my own pantry to create new life. Each day brings a new surprise.

My living sandwich is constantly changing. Watch out, Julia Child. There's a new chef in town!

TWENTY-ONE

GIVING ADVICE WITHOUT MAKING SUGGESTIONS

So is my word that goes out from my mouth:
It will not return to me empty, but will accomplish what I desire
and achieve the purpose for which I sent it.

—Isaiah 55:11

G iving advice is an art form. At least that's what I've been told.

For a select few, when they give advice, people sit up and listen. Heads nod in agreement as their words are taken to heart. Immediately suggestions are put into action. For the majority of us, however, no matter what we say or do, no one will ever follow our lead.

I am wondering what the difference might be. And I think the answer could be semantics and intent.

Giving advice is a response to a request. Someone seeks information, asks for, solicits, and is open to another point of view. Making suggestions is the antithesis. It comes in the form of unsolicited, unsought, and undesired advice, given freely and without restraint.

I confess that I am guilty of the latter and desirous of the former.

The Lord brought this truth home to me one day as I was driving across an overpass. Suspended above the ground, I looked down on an ocean of trees. I knew that just beneath this sea of green were houses, cars, Big Wheels, BBQ pits, baby toys, and more. Yet all I could see from the overpass were two church steeples, one high school cupola, and stadium lights—things of import standing head and shoulders above the fray. Then it hit me. Giving advice is like that, a visible reminder of what makes a difference in life. Making suggestions is more like the things below. They hide as a conglomerate of indistinguishable minutiae, overwhelming the senses when they rise to the surface at the same time.

Although grandmothers have few faults, the one we are most criticized for is our ability to make suggestions at inappropriate moments. What we really want to do is give advice, but somehow we reverse this process.

As a young mom, I remember painstakingly rearranging hand-me-downs and garage sale items in my home to produce an eclectic look. I took great pride in the *House and Garden* effect I had created. It would drive me crazy when my mother would visit and suggest a new place for the sofa, a new arrangement for the chairs, or a better placement for a picture. She was right, of course, but I would rather lose my left arm than admit it.

I find now that this is me. Many a hole has been bitten in my tongue as I struggle to keep my mouth shut. Far too many times my mouth has gotten away from me. Suggestions have a way of jumping out when I least expect them. Before I know it, I have blurted out another one. If only a mouth guard could be invented that would protect grandmothers from ourselves.

The day I learned the difference between advice and suggestions is forever etched in my memory. Darin, a recent college graduate, was planning a road trip, casting off for places unknown. No schedule, no timetable. I was helping him pack. I pulled out maps, file folders of historic sites, musts to see and do. Forget that he didn't ask. Of course he needed my help, my expertise. I conveniently forgot that thirty years earlier I had Eurailed my way through Europe on five dollars a day, just me and Gail, my college roommate. No tour, no itinerary. I sure didn't want any suggestions from my parents. And we survived.

I was standing in my office when he vented his frustration. "Mom, you are always telling me what to do. You and Dad never let me make up my own mind. You always have a better way, a better suggestion."

I'm sure he had said this before, but this time I actually *heard* it. He was right. In my eagerness to be a part of his process, I had jumped in headfirst, uninvited, throwing cold water on all his plans. I vowed then and there to never make suggestions to him again and told him so. Of course, I haven't been able to completely live up to this vow, but I've certainly tried. At least I have been more aware.

We made a covenant that day. I would no longer interfere in his life by making unsolicited suggestions, and he would no longer get angry if he asked for my advice but didn't like my response. I told him that if he did not want my advice, he better not ask. This was one of my all time touchstone moments—an "aha" experience.

I haven't yet perfected the art of giving advice, but I do think I am getting better. I have begun to recognize the outward signs when I make unwelcome suggestions. Shoulders stiffen, eyebrows rise, and smiles fade when I step into their worlds. Their attentiveness rises, however, when they solicit advice, and I give it lovingly and willingly. Now I am beginning to notice the faces of my grandchildren when their parents repeat this same generational faux pas. I find myself cringing. The scene is all too familiar, and it's not a pretty picture.

Giving advice or making suggestions, that is the question. I definitely don't want to leave a legacy of rising minutiae, of offering trivia at inopportune moments. I want to be remembered as a tower of strength, a cupola of wisdom, a light in the darkness that surfaces only when needed to bring a healing balm to open wounds.

In time, maybe I can learn to tether the tongue and think before I speak.

TWENTY-TWO

MAYDAY! MAYDAY!

Take courage! It is I. Don't be afraid.
—Matthew 14:27

L ife is full of surprises. I personally don't understand how people survive a crisis without a strong faith. Sometimes faith is the only thing we have to anchor us when the wind rages and the water rises.

Many years ago we had a time-share at the lake. One of my favorite pastimes was to sit on the deck, protected by a large overhang, and watch the storms as they made their approach. One of the things I noticed is that a storm comes up in one of two ways. Sometimes you see it from a distance. This kind of storm is expected and you are able to watch and prepare as it makes its way toward you.

Then there are the unexpected storms that seem to rise out of nowhere. You didn't see it coming. You've made no plans. It takes you by surprise. Most of the storms of life come in this fashion. You have no time to prepare. You only have time to send out a desperate cry for help. "Mayday! Mayday!" Trouble ahead.

One such storm happened in our life. Lily was born in May on a beautiful spring morning—such a beautiful, precious baby. What joy we felt as Jack and I baked a surprise cake for her family. We decorated the dining room and her bedroom with pink balloons and crepe paper. She was the first female born in our family since me. I just felt joy when I saw her. I described her as a child of joy to my friends.

After a few weeks, it became clear that Lily was not thriving. She was not a good eater and was diagnosed with reflux. Nothing seemed to agree with her. Everything the doctors tried did not seem to help. Before my very eyes, she seemed to be shrinking. She was not gaining weight, and yet she did not cry or whimper. I remember crying out to God for wisdom, for mercy, for help. "Mayday! Mayday!" I prayed over her. I know that Lee and Holly spent many a night in anguish, helpless in the face of an unseen enemy.

One day stands out for me as a turning point. As I sat with Lily, I sang songs and held her tight, thinking that if love could heal, surely she would get better. I looked into her little eyes and fully entrusted her to God. It was an excruciating moment.

I remember telling her, "Lily, we all love you. We hope you will stay with us. But it is your choice. It will be hard, but we will abide by whatever you decide."

Lily had all sorts of tests, and the prognosis that came back was grim. Lee and Holly were in shock and didn't know what to do. I had no wisdom, no experience, no idea how to comfort them.

"Mayday, Mayday!"

I remember standing in the hall with Holly, hearing the heart cry of a mother in pain searching for answers. All I could do was hold her as she cried. When she asked what she should do, I had no idea. All of a sudden an answer came, most definitely, divinely inspired. My daddy used to say, "You just have to keep on keeping on." I repeated this and added, "You know, we don't know what will happen. We don't know if the prognosis is correct or not. I think for now I would just treat her normal. We will surround her with love, and if their prediction manifests, we will deal with it at that time. You have lots of family and friends and support. We will all get through this together. I think I would not trust in the reports of man, but would wait and see what happens."

We cried together and began the job of waiting.

Lily crawled on Easter Sunday. What a testament to resurrection and new life. Holly was having the family for lunch.

It was a beautiful day, and we were sitting on a blanket in the front yard. I was taking pictures. Lily was fascinated with my camera. I laid it down on the blanket and was watching the beautiful morning unfold. The next thing I knew, she lurched forward and was after it. What a joyous moment on this day of promise.

Today, Lily is five. She is still very small for her age, but she is feisty. She is a delight and joy, and she continues to amaze us. She swims like a fish and is becoming more and more self-confident each day. She is reaching out to others, and her laughter often fills the room. It warms my heart when I see her run to the curb in front of my house and yell to the children across the street. "What is your name? Where is your house? Can I come and play?"

What a marvel God is. I thank him for the blessing that Lily brings into my life. I can't imagine my world without the joy that she brings. Who can trust in the reports of man? When the storms come, the question is not whether we will be swept away but whether we will stand firm in our faith, trusting that whatever the future holds, God will work all things together for good.

"Mayday! Mayday!"

And he comes. "Take courage! It is I. Don't be afraid."

My cup runneth over.

TWENTY-THREE

LISTENING WITH TWO EARS AND ONE HEART

He who walks with the wise, grows wise.
—Proverbs 13:20

As grandmothers, we have an important mandate to model the art of listening and the importance of following through to our grandchildren. Make no mistake—our grandchildren are watching us all the time. Our example is our most powerful tool.

Nothing is more meaningful to little eyes and ears than being heard. The skill of listening is important and very much underrated. In conversations, most of us are planning our next argument and don't even hear what others say. Or, as it is so often in my case, we are distracted and miss the gist of someone's heart. Jesus didn't miss anyone's heart. He heard what people said. He even heard what they were *really* saying, behind their words: "I thirst . . . I want to see . . . I want to be healed." He heard beyond the words to the heart of the matter and he gave life. He breathed hope and healing.

Do we? Do we really listen when our grandchildren tell us what they want or need?

Last week I took Lily to the mall just to spend time with her. I call it our "shop till we drop" time. She's only five, so what that means is that we do a lot of looking, and we do a lot of talking. We mainly browse, look, and feel.

On this particular day, we walked by a shop for kids. It wasn't really a beauty shop, but there were kids inside getting their hair punked and their nails done. Lily is not one to often try new things. She likes to watch and wait. Finally when she feels safe, she will try something new. On this day she bounced right into the shop and said, "I want to do it!"

She is very reserved and often painfully shy, so this was a bit out of character. I said, "Sure, why not," and off we went.

As I listened with my two ears and my one heart, I heard a child who has spent her life watching and holding back. Today, for whatever reason, she was willing to explore new territory. I was honored and blessed to be there. For Lily, this was a big step.

For me, it was a great adventure. Later, when I took her home, her family gave her positive feedback. She stood back and watched their reactions. When I got back to Fort Worth that night, Holly e-mailed a picture of Lily and James. They had spent hours making themselves up, dressing in costume— she as a punk rocker, he as a warrior. They put on a play for Holly and Lee. I was pleased that I had listened to Lily and helped provide an opportunity for an experience that benefitted the whole family.

By the same token, my grandson, James, is game for anything. One of his biggest fascinations is the car wash. Whenever he calls me, he says, "Marme, car dirty." This is code for "When you come to visit, will you take me to the car wash?" He wants his time too. We have now developed a routine. Chicken McNuggets at McDonalds followed by a trip to the car wash. We top the day off with an Eskimo pie for dessert. Listening with my two ears and one heart has created a time of sharing with this two-year-old that can't be replaced.

In addition to listening to what our grandchildren want and need, we also need to be attuned to their comments, to what they may be revealing about us and our own behavior. The lips of children can be powerful tools in our own transformations. At dinner one night, Jack was quoting Proverbs 14:29, which he had learned at Bible school: "A patient man has great understanding, but a quick-tempered man displays folly." My husband, Jim, asked him to explain what this meant.

Jack said, "You know, Big Dad. Like the other night when

you left dinner early to get ice cream when no one else was ready. You did not show patience."

Out of the mouths of babes. That certainly got my attention—and Jim's too. I know we are both watching our behavior more closely these days.

As a result, I have made a point to be more aware of my own impatience. I know Jim has been paying closer attention to his also. Transformation has occurred before my eyes. He seems to play more, laugh more, is more loving and more present. I have seen signs that he is listening with his two ears and his whole heart. I loved the day when he taught Jack how to ride a bicycle. They were in the driveway. I heard such a commotion that I ran to the door, and there he was, asking for the video camera, so proud I thought he was going to burst.

It warms my heart when I see this man with whom I have spent almost forty years get on the floor and wrestle with his grandsons or color the same picture over and over because Lily wants to direct him a certain way. I love to see him gently rock and cuddle newborn Strother or tuck two-year-old James into bed, answering his every question with love and patience. To hear the two of them whisper their stories in the dark, to hear their bedtime prayers, to later find them both asleep on the same pillow—it doesn't get any better than that.

God is good, indeed.

TWENTY-FOUR

ARE WE NOT A FAMILY ANYMORE?

I will pour out my Spirit on your offspring, and my
blessing on your descendents.
They will spring up like grass in a meadow, like poplar
trees by flowing streams.
—Isaiah 44:3-4

I grew up in a divorced family. My parents divorced when I was two, and my mother remarried when I was four, although as a child I never felt different. The only incident I remember was in junior high as I was flipping through my class directory. All the student names were listed alphabetically. Smith, John—parents . . . address . . . phone number. I noticed that my entry was longer, mainly because my parents' last name was different from mine. This didn't seem important to me at the time. Just another blip on my radar screen.

This first time I was aware that I might be different was in high school. I remember being shocked by a conversation with my gym teacher. As we stood in the gymnasium, she said to me, "You know, you are really very well-adjusted for a kid who comes from a broken home." She must have thought this was some sort of compliment.

Until that moment, I had never really thought much about my family. I definitely didn't think of my home as being broken. After all, it was a traditional family: Mom, stepdad, two brothers, and me. My life seemed normal and fairly stable, but somehow this comment put a knife in my heart.

At that moment, I realized I was a statistic.

Since that time I have seen many statistics in my office as a therapist, and I have discovered a very important truth. Children from divorced families need a stabilizing person in their lives, someone who assures them by word and deed that they are loveable. They need to be reassured that divorce is not their fault. They need to know there is nothing they did to cause divorce. Divorce is about parents, not children. Those who do not receive this assurance carry burdens that negatively affect their lives for years.

No, divorce is never easy at any age, but safety nets and safe havens can be created to help ease the effect on hurting lives.

There is a wonderful scene in the movie *Mrs. Doubtfire*. The main character is a lovely English granny on a children's television program. As she sits in an oversized wingback chair, she reads a letter delivered by the postman that morning:

Dear Mrs. Doubtfire,

Two months ago, my mom and dad decided to separate and not live in the same house. My brother Andrew says we are not to be a family anymore. Is this true? Am I to lose my family? Is there anything I can do to bring them back together?

Mrs. Doubtfire's response is wonderful and one we should all take to heart.

Dear Katie McKormick,

Some parents when they are angry get along better when they don't live together. Sometimes they don't get back together and sometimes they do. But don't blame yourself. Just because they don't love each other anymore doesn't mean they don't love you. There are many different kinds of families . . .

What words of wisdom. Every child from a broken home needs a Mrs. Doubtfire in his life. This person comes in all shapes and sizes. She can be an aunt, neighbor, or teacher, but more often than not, she is a grandmother. Many a weeping client reported that it was her grandmother who helped her develop her self-worth. It was her grandmother who affirmed the divorce was not her fault.

A grandmother's influence cannot be underestimated. Unfortunately, we can't change nor can we control the situations or the parents in our grandchildren's lives. We can't keep our grandchildren from becoming statistics of divorce. What we can do is affirm them through thick and thin. We can hold them close to our hearts, look in their eyes, and tell them that they have value. We can whisper to them that they are special, loveable, and truly loved by us. We can assure them that nothing they can ever do will cause us to divorce them.

Are we not to be a family anymore? Although the answer may be no, not a nuclear family, a resounding yes follows, for in our hearts we will always be a family.

My dear friend Deborah's life was cut short by cancer, yet her wisdom and legacy have made a huge impact on the world. She has definitely made an impact on me. "We are Velcroed at the heart," she used to say of her marriage. "That means that nothing, no, nothing, will ever tear us apart." I love that expression and have used it time and time again, substituting the term *grandchildren* for *marriage*.

They love it and know exactly what I mean. We will always be family. Nothing, no, nothing, will ever change that. Our hearts are stuck together forever.

PART 5

GRAND CONNECTIONS

TWENTY-FIVE

AN ENDANGERED SPECIES

Peacemakers who sow in peace raise a harvest
of righteousness.
—James 3:18

What do a nuclear family and a spotted owl have in common? Answer: they are both endangered species.

An endangered species is an animal that is almost extinct. Not many years ago, ecologists placed the spotted owl on the endangered species list. Over the years, with careful nurturing, patience, and care, the spotted owl has begun to return to its habitat.

Not so with the nuclear family—with father, mother, and children all living together. Each year, the number of nuclear families decreases with no change in sight. What is a person to do whose family has become endangered? What kind of care can be done to bring the family back into balance?

Becoming a peacemaker is one way to help. A healer of the breach can do much to heal the family. Families are hard enough, but building nonnuclear families takes a lot of work. Peacemaking is, clearly, easier said than done. To actively make a commitment to be a peacemaker is difficult. To paraphrase the *Life Application Bible*, too often we see peace as the absence of conflict, interpreting peacemaking as a passive act. But an effective peacemaker actively pursues peace.

Because peacemaking is a byproduct of commitment, peace is a result of healthy relationships. When problems are anticipated, they can be prevented. When conflict is brought out into the open, it becomes manageable.

When I was in the fifth grade, my daddy married a woman named Shirley, a five-foot-one Lauren Bacall look-alike. She was a character. Into low-fat eating before it was in vogue, she maintained a dancer's body until the day she died. To the astonishment of young and old alike, she could stretch her leg up the wall, just like a Broadway dancer. Her greatest disappointment was that she never had children. An emergency hysterectomy prevented that dream from becoming a reality.

Shirley developed Alzheimer's in the early 1990s. I had lost touch with her after my dad died, but my cousin George, a lawyer, advised her for many years. I suppose my neglect was partially a result of residual issues with her, due to her long-standing drinking problem. When I moved back to Fort Worth, Shirley's Alzheimer's was rearing its ugly head, and George contacted me. He needed help. Since I was the only child of my father, and since they had no children together, I was the logical one to step forward.

All peacemakers move to the front.

But would I be able to practice what I preached? Transitioning from anger and distance was not easy for me. Through much prayer and the grace of God, I was able to move forward in time toward forgiveness and caregiving.

Shirley lived a total of eleven years in an assisted living facility as well as in an Alzheimer's unit. During those years, we developed an amazing relationship. She was so childlike and loving and had a great sense of humor—sides I had not seen during her drinking years.

One of my favorite memories occurred the day she moved from her apartment into the assisted living facility. Always the Southern belle, she went to the beauty parlor in order to look her best. She returned with her hair in rollers. When I asked her about the rollers, she stated, "I want to look my best for my first meal in the dining room."

When the time came to go to the dining room, I was astounded when she refused. "I can't go to the dining room," she explained. "My hair is in rollers."

She kept those rollers in for three days. The nursing staff finally refused to bring any more food to her room. I laughingly drove back to Dallas to take the rollers out and help her make the adjustment.

She didn't know me the last two years, but at some level we still connected. Jim and I sat with her the day she died. We sang songs and read the Scriptures over her. She became peaceful and went faster than expected. I wished I had done more. Later, in what I consider a divine encounter, I spoke with a nephew, a young man I had never met. After describing her death, he relayed a story about the death of his own grandmother, Shirley's mom. In her final days, in the Southern tradition, the family called in a "dying nurse," probably the equivalent of today's hospice worker. She sat by the bedside, sang, and read Scripture. Although Shirley did not know me at the end, I believe she recognized that the dying nurse had come. It was time to go.

Yes, nuclear families are becoming an endangered species. But hope is not lost. There is always room for breathing life.

The spotted owl is on the rise. We would do well to patiently nurture and care for him in any way we can. If we do, he will no longer be endangered.

TWENTY-SIX

DO YOU HEAR WHAT I HEAR?

Be still, and know that I am God.
— Psalm 46:10

D o You Hear What I Hear?" has always been my favorite Christmas carol. I love the soft, gentle notes as they draw out the words: "Do you hear what I hear?"

I melt as the violins respond: "A song, a song high above the trees with a voice as big as the sea."

I love this carol because it is about listening, hearing the sounds of the night. The words challenge the heart to hear and know truth. The theme calls us to recognize that moment when truth manifests itself before us.

My friend Janina tells a story about listening. She gleaned this wisdom from a man who mentored his children in a quiet time each day. His example stressed the importance of sitting quietly, listening to what he called the song of the heart.

How many of us listen? How many know the song of the heart? How many teach our grandchildren to stop and listen?

Years ago, I initiated a rest time with my grandchildren. Each year, they come to spend time in the summer with me and Big Dad. Following the hectic morning activities, I usually set aside a time in the afternoon for rest. I call it our quiet time. Jack tells me that at his house they don't have quiet time, but I told him that at Marme's house we do. I wish I could say that I began this ritual for noble reasons, but I confess it was more a result of necessity. Tired and needing to regather strength, I did it for me. Now it has become a tradition.

Janina's story, however, includes a message for me to take to heart. During an extended visit, she decided to try a quiet time with her grandchildren. After she picked them up at school, she parked the car underneath an oak tree, rolled the windows down, and told them, "Now we are going to do something really fun. We are going to have a quiet time and listen."

Expectantly their faces lighted up in anticipation. She explained the plan, and wouldn't you know it, as soon as she stopped talking, a train went by. They listened. They clearly heard the whistle, the wheels as they clattered on the track, the sounds of the cars clanging together. The children were amazed and excited. When quiet time was over, they had much to talk about.

The next day they tried it again. This time they heard a bird singing and leaves rustling as the wind blew through the trees.

About two days later, Annie, age four, awoke in the early morning, crying. When asked what was wrong, Annie explained, "I miss my mommy." Janina asked her what could be done. "I need a quiet time for a few minutes," Annie replied, "so I can miss her."

Janina left the room. A few minutes later, Annie came down the hall. "I'm done," she said.

Something happened in those few minutes. In the way of a child, Annie listened to the song of her heart and was comforted. Perhaps she thought of her mom and her favorite memory. Maybe she cried and sucked her thumb or sang her favorite song. We don't know what transpired in those precious moments, but I would like to think that she heard a still, small whisper from a loving God who said, "It is OK. I am here."

I like the idea of connecting a quiet time to a time of listening to the song of the heart. I like encouraging my grandchildren to stop and listen, to regather and recenter when they have a need. Next summer I am going to adopt this expanded approach, using it as a springboard for a time of reflection and sharing with my own grandchildren.

Do you hear what I hear?

Not yet, but I am trying.

TWENTY-SEVEN

ONE, TWO . . . ONE, TWO, THREE

Let us come before him with thanksgiving
and extol him with music and song.
— Psalm 95:2

Stepgrandparenting is like the Texas two-step, always in motion. One often has to count the steps to keep up. One must keep the feet moving at all times.

One of the most exciting benchmarks of the early twenty-first century might be the renewed interest in dancing, brought about as a result of the TV show *Dancing with the Stars*. Secretly, I am hoping that history books will paint these years as the return to great dancing—a kind of Roaring Twenties, if you will.

Grandparenting, in general, is like a dance. Sometimes it moves too fast, sometimes too slow. Whether we dance a fox-trot, jitterbug, samba, or rumba, it is always a good idea for us grandmothers to learn the rules. Unfortunately, a stepgrandmother dances to an altogether different tune. She must be diligent in not only learning the rules but in sticking to them.

I have no experience in being a stepgrandmother, but I grew up with one, which gives me a different perspective. Perhaps my perception is skewed because it comes through the eyes of a child. But it doesn't hurt to learn from a child's paradigm to better perfect the dance.

Helen was my stepdad's mother, thus my grandmother by marriage. She was a wonderful lady who dressed to the nines, knitted her own sweaters, and wore charm bracelets that jingled when she walked. Every Christmas she joined us for Santa time. My stepdad, whom I called "Guppy," would call her at 5 a.m. and then make us wait for her behind a swinging door to the dining room. In our eager anticipation, it seemed like it took forever for her to dress and drive the few blocks to our house! By the time she arrived, we had worked ourselves into a frenzy. Every year her gift to me was a hand-knit sweater with the label "By Helen with Love." How I wish I had kept those treasures. What might they be worth today—materially and emotionally!

As a child, I always wondered if my grandmother Helen felt differently about me than she did my brothers. There just was something different about our relationship. Outwardly, she was warm and loving to me, but I always wondered. There is no doubt that she would be horrified to hear me voice this sentiment, but as a child, this is what I perceived. I conjectured that it might be because I was the only female. As I grew older, I thought it might have to do with the divorce, which was not as common in those days as it is now. It was definitely not discussed openly.

Possibly I carried this baggage far longer than I needed to. Whether my perceptions were correct or not, I will never know. I wish I had voiced my concerns. I wonder if other children of that age have the same insecurities.

Today there are few families without some sort of blending or step-something. Thank goodness the attitude toward them is different. I am grateful that divorce and stepgrandparenting are more openly discussed, that children have safe outlets for their concerns. I am amazed at the creativity and ingenuity of the stepgrandmothers I know. Turning up the music, they have a lot of dance inside, a lot of love to give. I am grateful to see it pouring out on grandchildren and stepgrandchildren alike.

My friend Bev is the best stepgrandmother I know. First and foremost, she has determined the importance of a good relationship with her stepgrandchildren's mothers, and she is clear to follow their rules and not make waves. Her house is a safe place to gather, and all are welcome at her table. She makes a point to do individual activities with all of her grandchildren, one of the things I have filed in my "hold till needed" folder. I love that she does not differentiate between grandchildren and stepgrandchildren. Every year she plans a special day of lunch and shopping with her teenage stepgranddaughter as an end-of-year celebration. She has a scrapbook full of these memories. She also has become a soccer grandmom as her stepgrandson is really into soccer. She sits on the sidelines in rain and snow, cheering on the team. And to top it off, she rents a house every year in Colorado for the summer, inviting all the kids and grandkids, step or otherwise, to pick a week to come and visit.

Today there are many books that offer ideas for stepgrandparenting, but each grandmother has to customize ways to bring her own stepgrandchildren on board. I suspect it gets harder as the children get older, but most grandmothers are not without invention. With the music in our hearts and the collection of old records in our attics, there's probably not a dance we can't master.

Rumba or jitterbug, stepgrandmothers are on the move!

TWENTY-EIGHT

A TRIANGLE IS THE SUM OF ITS ANGLES

Let the wise listen and add to their learning,
and let the discerning get guidance.

—Proverbs 1:5

Most of us learned about geometry in high school. A triangle is the sum of its angles. If you add A plus B plus C, you get 180 degrees.

To be honest, I never really liked geometry. Which brings me to an important lesson: nothing good comes from triangles. I believe they are to be avoided at all costs. One does not want to get involved in any type of triangle—especially one that involves a husband, child, and child's spouse.

Then how do triangles develop?

Triangles are a result of poor communication. Often people are not willing to communicate directly with one another.

For reasons unknown, they seek a safer venue from which to converse.

The year Lee left for college, I came face to face with triangles in my own family. I remember the evening perfectly. We were sitting in our usual places at the dinner table. I don't remember the topic, but I am sure it was typical dinner conversation: "How was your day? What did you do at school today?"

I talked about whatever moms talk about. Out of the blue, Darin said, "Mom, now that Lee is in college, I am not going to translate for you and Dad. If you want him to know something, you will have to tell him yourself."

Without even knowing it, Jim and I were involved in a triangle. The therapeutic term is triangulation, people talking to one another through a third party—in this case, our son Darin.

Triangulation is an easy habit to fall into. Awareness is the key to the cure. Most families do it all the time, without even thinking. One thing is certain: if we do it with our kids, you can bet we will do it with our grandkids.

It is imperative that we determine if this is a family trait we want to pass down. If the answer is no, behavior must be changed, posthaste.

Changing the paradigm of triangles is important. For

Jim and me, it was not easy. After many years of thoughtful attentiveness, a separation, and a recommitment in our marriage, I think we are finally making progress.

My granddaughter Lily has taught me a lot about triangles—how to study them from a different angle, how to deal with them in creative ways.

Lily is studying triangles in school. She loves to draw them in crayon, marker, pencil, or using her Stencil Master. We find them everywhere. Recently we have expanded our repertoire, drawing squares for houses and triangles for roofs. Triangles also make good eyes and noses in pumpkins, skirts on girls, and hats on snowmen. We have found many creative ways to draw triangles.

Being creative in communication follows the same rules as geometry. Learning to draw a straight line from A to B is much more beneficial and quicker than triangulating. As parents and grandparents, it is up to us to begin making this change. If we don't do it, no one else will.

I always thought of myself as a triangle growing up. On side A, I had my mother, Guppy, and brothers. On side C—Daddy, Shirley, and his family. I was pretty much side B, right in the middle. This last year, for the first time, instead of triangulating, I had the opportunity to draw a straight line from A to B to C.

As with most serendipitous moments, it happened in an unexpected way. My dad's side of the family and I share a love for the same area of Colorado. Last year my cousin George was there at the same time as my mother and brothers, and we invited him to have dinner with us. As I sat on the porch and listened to my family visiting with one another, I marveled at the miracle of it all: the ease with which they addressed each other, the laughter that spontaneously filled the room—it was as if they had known each other for years. I stood in awe of a God who would draw the two halves of my family together in such a unique way as to make my life a perfect whole. What once had been triangulated was now complete. If I had tried, I could not have orchestrated a more perfect union. The line was now straight. No more triangles for me.

A triangle is the sum of its angles. This formula works well for geometry, but I am glad there are no more triangles in my life. Pack it up and straighten it out. I'll take a straight line every time.

TWENTY-NINE

LOVE IS EASIER THE SECOND TIME AROUND

By this all men will know that you are my disciples, if
you love one another.

—John 13:35

F rank Sinatra was right: love is easier the second time around. Being a grandmother is taking these words and personifying them ten times over.

I always wondered what moving into the next phase of life would be like. Now I know. It's like being an Oreo cookie. After you take off the outer covering, the good stuff is inside.

My grandchildren love Oreos. They insist on having their own glasses of milk, filled to the perfect spot for dunking. Chocolate crumbs scatter on the top of the milk as the cookies absorb just the right amount of moisture.

As a child, I didn't know about dunking cookies in milk, but as an adult, I have perfected the art form. Likewise, as a young adult, I didn't know much about parenting, but as a grandmother, I have perfected the art form of grandparenting. All it takes is love.

How blessed I am to experience so many Oreos in my life. I get to sit down and dunk my cookies without the hassle. No going to the store, getting out the dishes, loading the dishwasher, cleaning the counter, changing the clothes, washing the clothes. I get to do all the good stuff and ignore the bad. Just dunking and eating and loving. It doesn't get any better than that.

The fun stuff is mine for the asking. From decorating the Christmas tree to playing golf to buying ice cream with cookie dough on top, I get to pick and choose.

This year we decorated the Christmas tree with all four grandchildren, plus my mother. What an adventure. Ornaments, lights, cheese, and crackers were scattered hither and yon. None of it fazed my mother, Cecca. She has perfected the art of loving. I am learning from her.

The angel that Lily wanted to put on the top of the tree was too heavy. The branch leaned precariously close to toppling the tree. What did I care? All the ornaments were arm's length high. I didn't even blink an eye. James put all his ornaments on the same branch. Yet it was the most beautiful tree I had ever seen. Strother just ate and slept in his bouncy seat—a little angel snoozing away. What a joy.

Yes, decorating the Christmas tree was much easier the second time around.

A friend told me that grandchildren are a second chance at life. I believe her. On the first try, I was not only learning, but I had to be disciplinarian, teacher, tutor, and parent all in one. The second time around I just get to love—children and grandchildren alike. The most fun part is I get to watch my children as they parent and improve on my mistakes. Their creativity amazes me.

Jim and I have been working with Jack on the art of negotiating. On a Thanksgiving visit to Fort Worth, the laundry was bulging with typically muddy clothes. Lee offered to pay Jack twenty-five cents to fold the laundry. Jack looked at him and said, "How about two dollars?"

Jack is a quick study. Lee reported that his first negotiation occurred a few weeks earlier and involved washing the car. As part of his weekly chores, Jack's responsibility is to wash the car. Lee pays him two dollars more if he washes the second car.

Jack loves math and is very good at it. Using observation and deductive reasoning, he began to question: "Dad, how much do you pay to go through the car wash?" Quickly he calculated that he was getting ripped off by only getting paid two dollars. He immediately negotiated Lee up to six dollars on the spot. Thank goodness he didn't know that two dollars is below the minimum wage. Now he is negotiating everything. I would like to think that Big Dad and I had a small hand in this situation.

I had not realized the full extent of second-time-around advantages until Strother was born. After four grandchildren, I realize how experienced I have become at grandparenting. I get to see my newest grandchild a lot. They drop him off for an hour or two or for an evening. Part of my second-time-around manual says to keep my mouth shut, learn their ways, and follow their patterns. My role is purely backup, here to help, but I am getting a firsthand glimpse of them as they grow in their parenting roles. What a blessing to observe them grow so beautifully and gracefully. They are a great team.

Darin tells a wonderful second-time-around story about Jim's dad. Lee was fifteen and learning to drive with a learner's permit. Darin wanted to drive too. Without permission, he backed his grandad's pickup out of the garage, scraping the fender in the process. Afraid to fess up, he kept his mouth shut. Through the process of elimination, Grandad figured out the culprit. He took Darin aside, sat him down, and told him, "You need to know, son, how much I love you. There is nothing you can't tell me. There is nothing you have done, or will ever do, that will keep me from loving you. You are my grandson, and I will always love you."

Darin experienced second-time-around, unconditional, grandparent love—and he has never forgotten it.

Love is, indeed, easier the second time around. Not easier because I love my grandkids more but because, somewhere in the process of life, I have learned more about love.

How blessed I am to be around to experience it.

THIRTY

WHEN THE ROLL IS CALLED UP YONDER

But you are a shield around me, O LORD;
you bestow glory on me and lift up my head.

—Psalm 3:3

D eath is a dirty word in the twenty-first century. Not only do we not deal with it, but we also run for cover whenever it is mentioned. Most of all, we keep our children as far away from it as possible.

The truth is we all are going to die. Like it or not, death is inevitable. One day the roll will be called up yonder, and our names will be on the list. I want to be ready, and I want my family to be ready. Rather than shield my grandchildren from death, I want to take advantage of the opportunity to deal with it head-on. Teaching them about death and dying is an important legacy to leave them.

My grandmother Shakey, great-grandmother Gangy, and

my dad died when I was away at school. I simply woke up one day and heard the news that they were gone. And Maman died when I was five. So I had no real experience with prolonged terminal illness. Guppy's death was the first I experienced on a daily basis, up close and personal.

He died of lung cancer. Having had two previous heart attacks, he surmised that his heart would get him. He had not counted on cancer. I have heard people speak of cancer as a gift. I don't know if I would go as far as to agree with that statement, but I will say that his illness was truly a sweet time in our family—a time of healing and love, of dealing with unfinished business.

He was ready. He knew it was his time, and he wanted to talk about it. Few were willing, uncomfortable with the topic. I was timid but willing. Every afternoon I sat with him in his outdoor sanctuary, and we talked. I watched as he prepared himself, opening up the window to his heart. We had wonderful conversations of angels and heaven, what it would be like, who had gone before. My perspective on death was forever changed.

As the day drew near, his spirit knew. "I think it'll be in about a week now," he said, as we sat on the patio in the warm sun. "You know, it's not really so bad."

"Well, it sure looks bad from here," I protested.

"Not really," he said. "What is hard is watching all of you as you struggle."

He was right on.

Jim's mom was the first of his parents to go. No one expected that she would be first. She was strong willed and determined to take care of her husband to the end. Her body just finally wore out; she had no reserve left. I am sure she is in heaven now, waiting at the front door with a pan of corn-bread and a pot of black-eyed peas on the stove. Even though her name was called first, I like to think that she went ahead with joy, to get their house in order.

About a week before she died, Jack and Lily came to visit. On the way to Sunday school, we stopped by for Jim to run in and check on his mom. Out of nowhere Jack insisted, "I want to see Grandmother. Big Dad went up, I want to go too." I have never seen him so adamant.

There is something healing in being able to say good-bye. A child's heart sometimes knows what adults cannot acknowl-edge. I believe he knew and wanted to say good-bye. Without fear, at the age of six, he walked right up to the bed and told her good-bye.

I don't know if my nephews really got to tell Guppy good-bye during his last days. I do know that after he died, Teddy made a wooden cross in honor of his grandfather and put it in the backyard. I suspect it was his way of saying good-bye, of grieving the loss of a legend.

I have observed a grace that is given during the dying process. We need only open our eyes to see it. Guppy died exactly one week after our conversation on the porch. His spirit knew, and God in his mercy was gracious. Guppy died on a summer's eve, throwing kisses to his family.

Jim's dad was gifted with amazing clarity on the day Jim's mom died. At one point he reported seeing angels as her time drew near. Out of the blur of dementia, he knew what needed to be done. Picking up a piece of paper from the bed-side table, he asked Darin to read it aloud. In retrospect, Lee has interpreted this action as a sign that he wanted to pray. Turning to his grandson was the only way he knew how. The paper said, "We gather together to ask the Lord's blessing. He chastens and hastens his will to make known."

To this day we have no idea where that paper came from.

God's grace was in great supply that day. In a moment of divine inspiration, Jim's wisdom and gentleness astounded me as he led his father in the letting-go process. "Dad," he said as he gently took him by the hand, "Mom has died. Soon they will take her away, and we won't see her again. If you want to, you need to sit by the bed and say good-bye to her."

The heart knows the things of import. As the three of us

watched, this man who could barely put a sentence together sat down, took her hand, and poured out a heart of love that could rival Shakespeare.

Yes, we will all die someday. I plan to be prepared. I plan to be ready, surrounded by those I love holding my hand as I make the transition from this life to the next.

When the roll is called up yonder, not only will I be ready, but I'll be there.

PART 6

GRAND GIFTS

THIRTY-ONE

SOMETHING BORROWED, SOMETHING BLUE

By wisdom a house is built,
and through understanding it is established;
through knowledge its rooms are filled
with rare and beautiful treasures.

—Proverbs 24:3–4

I love antiques, especially early Texan. I love that someone once loved these things, that they have been part of another lifetime. I love that they have a history. I wish I knew their stories. In contrast to today's throw-away mentality, I love that they have the possibility of being refurbished and reused. I love their potential and patina. I love that I am just a pass-through in their existence and, for a time, can enjoy their luster.

Antiques are a metaphor for aging—time and space borrowed for a season. Like antiques, we have a moment in time to make a difference. Aging is our time to shine, a season for splendor, and an opportunity to better our world. We are a pass-through to another generation.

Last year Jim and I remodeled our kitchen and bought a new refrigerator, stainless steel with a freezer on the bottom instead of the top. They certainly don't make them like they used to. I am stunned at the difference. This will definitely not be an antique to be passed down to the next generation.

In contrast, a few months ago I found an old icebox in my in-laws' basement. Now that is a refrigerator. I plan to refinish it and use it for storage. I do have experience at refinishing antiques. Ironically, our very first furniture purchase as a married couple was an old-timey, one-door icebox. Jim found it in someone's front yard and bought it for five dollars. We rebuilt it, paneled the inside, and used it for a bar. Today that refrigerator sits in Darin's house. Refurbished, refinished, and reused—an antique that shines as a reminder of life and history.

Clothes and memories also have the opportunity to be refurbished. When Blythe was planning her wedding, she decided to forgo the traditional wedding with all the trimmings. She was adamant about not wearing a wedding dress. She had high hopes of wearing her grandmother's blue velvet cocktail suit in which she was married during WWII. It turned out that October in Texas was a bit too hot for velvet, but it got me thinking. The sentiment is admirable. Refurbished, refinished, reused—something to pass down to the next generation.

"Something borrowed, something blue" is an apt description of grandmothers. We've been around the block. Like antiques, we may be old, but we have lots of potential. What an opportunity to pass down a legacy. Surely we have something blue in our storehouses that can be borrowed or passed down. And most definitely our knowledge and wisdom count for something.

Recently my mother and I went through her scrapbooks. Ever since Guppy died, she has been overwhelmed by all the pictures and paraphernalia. She can't decide what to do with them. What a treasure. Looking through his scrapbook—letters, WWII pictures, his father's WWI letters, and his journal from the year he spent working in the bush in Africa—I learned so much about him, his life, and his history. I wish I had spent more time talking to him about these things, more time listening and learning about him and his uniqueness. I hope to take the opportunity today to listen to my mom while I still have the time.

Our things, whether antique or not, will be passed on anyway, whether in or out of our control. Hopefully we will take the time to discover the lessons from our ancestors. Surely we will recognize the value of the antiques in our possession.

Hopefully our children will see the value of us—antiques that we are—and learn.

Refurbished, refinished, reused. Thank goodness we stand tall, a monument and reminder of the heritage of before and the possibility of after.

THIRTY-TWO

CUSTOMIZING KEEPSAKES

Therefore every teacher of the law who has been
instructed about the kingdom of heaven is like the
owner of a house who brings out of his storeroom new
treasures as well as old.

—Matthew 13:52

Life is full of keepsakes. Every person has them. Every person keeps them. You find them in closets, in scrapbooks, under beds, and in garages. Keepsakes are forever.

Recently we cleaned the house my in-laws lived in for more than fifty years. Talk about keepsakes: the rehearsal dinner dress my mother-in-law wore in 1963, Pat O'Brien glasses from the weekend Jim and I got pinned, a Monmouth Duo blanket, Jim's Eagle Scout badge, and Jim's dad's arrowhead collection. As best I could tell, they had not thrown anything away in the past sixty-five years. The house was bulging at the seams.

It got me thinking. What is a keepsake? The thesaurus gives synonyms for *keepsakes*: reminders, mementos, testimonials, relics, trophies. But I'm not sure these words adequately describe a keepsake. To me, a keepsake is something that when I look at it, my mind is flooded with the taste, smell, sound, and memory of an event. It is something that I don't have to write an explanation for in the scrapbook. I know that the program from *My Fair Lady* was the night my daddy took me to dinner and dancing at the Adolphus Hotel. I know that the silver bracelet in my jewelry box is the one that jingled late at night when my mother tucked me in after returning from an evening out.

In the process of cleaning, I found a closet stuffed with antique quilts. Now those are keepsakes. In fact, I bet both of his grandmothers, as well as his mom and aunts, helped make them. I am blessed to have such treasures in my possession. As I review the contents of my home, I see that the majority of my furniture belonged to my grandparents. They are true treasures, and I am flooded with memories every time I walk past them. In my living room stands the desk where my grandmother Shakey spent hours playing solitaire. I can still see her sitting in her chair, turning the cards, reshuffling the deck. In my entry hall, her clock plays the same comforting chimes I remember hearing as a young child when I would have a sleepover at her house. In my living room is a dry sink that stood in my daddy's entry hall. At Christmas, I use my grandmother Maman's china. These are real keepsakes.

I began to notice other people's keepsakes. My friend Belinda's house is filled with art painted by her mother. Megan's house also is filled with knickknacks and treasures from her mother's house. A crocheted afghan adorns her bed, covering her home and her heart with memories. Upstairs, Mary Ellen has artwork that belonged to both grandparents and a bed that belonged to her great-grandmother. At his wedding, Linda's son knelt on a pillow made of fabric from his maternal grandmother's wedding dress. At my own wedding, my hat was covered with fabric from Shakey's wedding dress—keepsakes, each and every one.

All of this to say, keepsakes are important. As grandmothers we are in unique positions to hand down those special items that have memories attached, whether they be material or spiritual, to those we love.

My goal is, at some point in time, to start giving my things away until I come out even at the end. One of the first things I learned when I married into a rural family was the concept of "coming out even." This phrase is often used in reference to a plate of food. If you are a really good eater and time things perfectly, you will end up with one bite of each item left on your plate at the end of a meal. This is coming out even. If I come out even on the day I die, it means all my things will be almost gone, shared with those I love.

I haven't quite figured out how I am going to do this, but it certainly is a nice thought. At least, I can begin to give some thought to what I cherish, what might be special to my family members, and make plans accordingly. That way I can customize my keepsakes for everyone and come out perfectly on the last day. At least, they will think I am a good planner.

Who could ask for more than that?

THIRTY-THREE

A HOPE CHEST

Whoever drinks the water I give him will never thirst.
Indeed, the water I give him will become in him a
spring of water welling up to eternal life.
—John 4:14

When I was in high school, my mother and brother, Ted, made a hope chest for me. They refurbished an old steamer trunk that belonged to my grandmother Helen and looked like it might have come over on the *Mayflower*. I love that chest. Ted painted it gold and covered it with red, blue, and green flowers. I certainly didn't have a trousseau, but from time to time I put a linen tablecloth or a handkerchief inside. More than anything, it was a reminder of the hope of promised things to come. Today I still have that hope chest. I can't bear to give it away, so it sits as a visible reminder of the hope of marriage and life that I had within me.

Today I don't need a physical hope chest. I have a spiritual hope chest that lives inside me that I carry wherever I go. In this chest I lay up my hopes and dreams, my expectations and secret desires. It is here that I will store the prayers of the heart, the dreams of eternity.

In my office I have two storage boxes: one marked *Lee*, the other marked *Darin*. Anytime I receive something that is meaningful from them or their family, I throw it in that box. Someday when I am gone, I hope that this box will be a physical reminder of all the moments, long since forgotten, when they were thoughtful and present. These boxes are overflowing, filled with their words and actions that touched my heart.

As I plan my spiritual hope chest, I can see that it, too, is close to overflowing with so much inside: dreams for my kids and grandkids, expectations for my own life. Like a fountain filled to the brim, it will overflow.

One summer Jim and I took a road trip through Tuscany. One of the most welcoming sights in each village was the fountain that sits in the middle of the square. There was never a time day or night that someone was not there drawing water, drinking from its abundance, or just being refreshed by the cool water.

That's how I feel. Just like that fountain, I am so full of love that it sort of flows out of me. Sometimes I can't seem to stop it. I hope that I am like that fountain, constantly healing and refreshing those with whom I come in contact. I pray that I am never too busy to pay attention to all who need refreshment. I seek to not hoard but pour out my abundance.

One of my favorite Bible verses is 1 Peter 3:15, which tells us to be prepared to give an answer to anyone who asks about our hope within. I love the admonishment about always being gentle and kind in our answer. Oh, that I would be like that fountain, standing firm in my faith, always available for one in need, offering a place of kindness and safety should anyone ask.

For my sixtieth birthday, Jim gave me a fountain for the backyard, a small version of the Italian experience. It is my new hope chest, a gentle reminder of the hope within me, the living water that continues to flow both day and night. Each time I look at it, I am reminded of this gift.

My grandchildren are also reminders of this hope within me. Strother, at six months, is discovering his voice, experimenting with different sounds and decibels. When he smiles, his life overflows. The gurgling and cooing of new life is a physical reminder of this living water overflowing. As he discovers the world around him—his feet, his toys, his "fa fa"—he overflows my world and fills my hope chest with joy.

Yes, I have a hope chest, and, yes, it is spiritual. It is inside me. Already it is overflowing. But unlike a physical hope chest, I don't think I will ever rebuild or replace it. Instead I will just allow God to create a larger space within me to hold more hope, a larger container that will continue to overflow onto my grandchildren.

After all, what are a few more pounds? How much can hope really weigh?

THIRTY-FOUR

HISTORY 101 AND MORE

Blessed are eyes that see what you see. For I tell you that
many prophets and kings wanted to see what you see but did
not see it, and to hear what you hear but did not hear it.

—Luke 10:23-24

All of us have a history. Whether it includes a shaded past or a long line of amazing inventions, we each have a legacy to pass on to our grandchildren. Our families have histories, too, and there is no one more qualified to be the family historian than the grandmother extraordinaire!

Children and grandchildren are fascinated by stories. I confess that I am not adept at remembering family history, but Aunt Martha and my husband are great at it. Shakey was the best. She used to regale my brothers and me with stories of my mother and her three siblings when they were young. They got into more trouble. Their antics were a great balm to us and cleansed our consciences. They experienced numerous traumas and family situations. To this day I am still impressed by Shakey's positive attitude toward trial and tribulation, and I credit any optimism I have as an inheritance from her.

When Jim and I were cleaning out his parents' home, Darin and Blythe discovered a trunk of pictures in the basement filled with Jim's maternal grandmother's memorabilia. They were fascinated as Jim took them on a trip down memory lane. He had amazing recall of life in the country in the '40s and '50s. This was highly significant, as was sitting at the kitchen table in his paternal grandparents' house—a house in the process of being handed down to us and, in time, to our sons, the fourth generation. They could not fail to see this generational connection.

My memory of family history is not as good as Jim's. But research and creativity is where I shine. It is important to apply my skills accordingly.

Last year I made a scrapbook for my mother's eightieth birthday called Eight Decades of Cecca. I traced her life from birth through the births of her four great-grandchildren. It was not surprising that she enjoyed the scrapbook, but I was surprised at the response of her grandchildren. As a young girl, she was a real beauty (and still is), and her athleticism, creativity, and sense of humor shone on every page. From tennis to swimming to dancing, her popularity was apparent. Each picture generated questions about life in "the good old days." Seeing a side of their grandmother previously unknown broadened their perspective and generated much storytelling and memory making. For me, it cemented the importance of keeping family history alive. I had never appreciated my mother's interest in genealogy before. Her diligent compilation of family letters and diaries is a gift that cannot be replicated; it can only be generation breathed. Hopefully, as I continue to age, I will pick up the mantle and carry forth her wonderful example.

In a world of instant gratification and electronic communication, it would serve our families well if we chose to make it one of our life goals to keep our family histories alive. The Bible is a great model for the recording of history, and we would do well to imitate its inspiration and accuracy. For Jim's father's eightieth birthday, he compiled a collection of essays his father had written about his childhood and had them bound in a book. Every member of our family received a copy. The conversations that have been generated by that book have broadened our family dynamics in new ways.

I hope that someday my grandchildren will be as fascinated with my history as my children have been with their grandparents' histories. As historians extraordinaire, we not only have the opportunity but also the duty to pass our history on to our progeny. As we become the elders of our generation, we have the unique opportunity to give our grandchildren living legacies that no one else can give them—parts of ourselves to remember, parts of their histories to hold on to forever.

THIRTY-FIVE

HEAR NO EVIL, SEE NO EVIL, SPEAK NO EVIL

*Let your conversation be always full of grace, seasoned
with salt, so that you may know how to answer everyone.*
—Colossians 4:6

E veryone remembers the story of the three little monkeys. The first little monkey has his hands over his ears. The second little monkey covers his eyes. The third little monkey has a protective guard over his mouth. Hear no evil, see no evil, speak no evil. As grandmothers, we would do well to heed these admonishments—especially the third little evil, the power of the tongue.

I know that as a wife, mother, and now grandmother, I have a lot to say. I have a lot I hear and see, things I want to speak about at the first opportunity. The problem is that no one wants to hear it, especially if it is unsolicited. So I am learning about discernment: when to speak and when to

keep silent . . . when to share what I see and when to be blind
. . . when to comment and when to become deaf and mute.

My daughters-in-law have been great instructors. I get to see
myself through their eyes through my ongoing and developing relationships with them. I am learning to see how my
actions and words affect others constructively and destruc-
tively. These are not easy lessons for me, and I have certainly
learned the hard way.

I have termed my speaking and acting without thinking as
walking into *uninvited territory* and running into a *land mine*.
My children have helped me develop working definitions for
these terms.

Uninvited territory, loosely defined, is an area in their lives,
not mine, that is not secure—an area into which I have not
been invited. *Land mine* is pretty self explanatory. One mis-
step and I'm toast. What is important to recognize is that land
mines cause explosions. My overall goal is to avoid explosions—at all costs. But most importantly, I must never, ever
throw hand grenades.

The good news is that, over the years, I have noticed that
the circumference of my uninvited territory is shrinking. I
seem to be invited in more often than in years past. In retrospect, I can see that they wanted me to wait until they gave
the invitation.

I remember how sensitive I was as a young mother, when my own mother and mother-in-law stepped off the path and into my territory. The same goes for me. When I step in to my children's lives without an invitation, I almost always step on a land mine, and everything falls apart for a while. Sometimes there might even be permanent damage, and that is to be avoided at all cost.

Recently my coffee group learned an important lesson about discernment. For the past ten years, six of us have met weekly to share our hearts and our lives as we process, listen, and learn from one another. A more loving and supportive group of friends one could never find. We lost our beloved Anita to cancer in 2001, so now we are five. We miss her terribly.

On this particular morning, Carolyn was sharing a family situation. She was in process, seeing with new clarity, reaching new conclusions. As is our custom, we let her talk, not offering advice or suggestions but letting her process to reach her own conclusions.

As she gained new insight and reached new conclusions, Courtney, who had had a previous appointment, came in late. She joined in the conversation, as we all often do, without hearing the beginning of the discussion. She kind of stepped on a land mine. As she had not been there from the beginning to see the process as it unfolded, she was totally taken by surprise. We all were taken by surprise.

This experience turned out to be a divine opportunity for us all—a lesson in trust and friendship. In a spirit of honesty, we talked through what had happened. By the grace of God, a giant explosion was avoided, and I marveled at how far we had come over the years. No one took offense, and friendships remained intact. Our dynamic as grandmothers allowed us to share our wisdom, perceptions, and understanding in a spirit of love. This was a one-hundred-and-eighty-degree turn for me, and a turning point on the grandmother journey to maturity.

That day we learned discernment. We reached down into our storehouse of knowledge to determine the times and seasons. We carefully maneuvered around "land mines" and "uninvited territory." We grew and are still friends. I couldn't help but pray that the lessons learned in the circle of friendship could be transposed into the family setting.

I was tested a few months later. On a monthly visit to Austin, Jack shared a problem he was having with a boy on the school bus who teased him every day. We discussed his options and then prayed about it. When I prayed, I asked for guidance for Jack's little problem. When the prayer ended, Jack corrected me.

"Marme," he said, "this is not a little problem. It is a big problem."

That is when I knew I needed to speak up. This was a big deal to him. It was clear he was reaching out, so I asked permission to share it with his daddy. He agreed. When I told Lee, he received it with a sense of caution, thinking Jack was playing to my sympathies. I spoke up boldly, for I had discerned that the issue needed addressing. Lee took the ball and ran with it. After further investigation, it turned out that the problem was, indeed, real, and they were able to resolve it as a family.

It felt good to be a part of the solution, to discern the need and to speak up, even risking criticism from my own son. I was glad that I had acted as an advocate for my grandson. I was also glad that my son had heard me. We were all pleased that the problem was resolved to everyone's satisfaction.

Hear no evil . . . see no evil . . . speak no evil. I don't have these three down yet, but I am learning. Hopefully this little monkey won't be a fool too many more times in the process.

THIRTY-SIX

FOR BETTER OR WORSE, FOR RICHER OR POORER

What we have heard and known,
what our fathers have told us.
We will not hide them from their children;
we will tell the next generation.
—Psalm 78:3-4

Where there's smoke, there's fire. Where there's a grand-mother, there's a story.

We all have stories and, for better or worse, they are ours. I often wonder what would happen if our children really knew our stories, really knew our lives. Would they be surprised by our choices? Would they grieve our mistakes? Would they honor our victories? Might our struggles and dreams, our successes and failures, somehow help heal some of the disappointments in their own lives? Could they learn from our mistakes? Would they see generational sin being passed down to them? If they knew, would they choose to do things differently?

Often I have pondered the life stories portrayed in movies such as *The Notebook* and *Message in a Bottle*. As I consider the deep love, commitment, romance, faithfulness, infidelity, life decisions, and healing of relationships that are depicted, I cry. I am aware that these are stories of people's lives, their histories, mistakes, and successes. But are they really that different from our own?

The problem is that most of us think we don't have stories. I mean real stories: ones that might speak to our children and grandchildren in their deep places, ones that might open eyes to potential pitfalls or alter the direction of their lives. Yet we were young once, had dreams, courted, fell in love, and began our lives together with our husbands. Yes, we each have stories to share.

If I am honest, I have to admit that for years I never thought much about my own parents' stories. It was fun to hear them tell of some of their adventures, their escapades. Those we knew by heart. But did we really know the depths of who they were? Did we really understand how they had become who they are today? Did we ever wonder how they got there?

It was not until I made my mother's scrapbook that I began to take a closer look at her. As I selected pictures representative of her life, I saw the person she used to be—a younger reflection of who she is today, a person with experiences I knew nothing about. I saw pictures of her and my dad before they divorced, holding hands, laughing, preparing to plant the gleam in their eyes that was me. They were people with hopes and dreams, a life that is part of my own history.

I have been through many life seasons myself. As Jim and I transition through these phases, individually and together, we have grown together as one. Yet there was a time in our own marriage when we almost divorced: a time of great pain, of soul searching, of forgiveness and rebuilding. For better or worse, do our children know about these times?

I remember sitting in the backyard with my mother in the middle of Jim's and my separation. I was grieving, hurt, confused—searching to find my way. She spoke up in favor of marriage. At one point, she said, "Well, you can't get divorced. In our family we don't get divorced!"

I looked at her in astonishment. "But, Mom," I said, "you got divorced."

Her response: "Oh yes, I did, didn't I?"

At that moment, I knew I didn't know anything about my mother's story, about the pain she had gone through, about the way she had handled that pain. I had no idea about the choices she had been forced to make. If she had shared her story with me, I wonder if I would have gained insight. I wonder if her mistakes were being passed on to me.

I once asked her how she thought her second marriage was different from her first. "I think you probably try harder," she said. "I think you become more accepting and expect less. You become more forgiving and more tolerant of imperfection." I know that's what happened in my own marriage after our time of separation and reconciliation. It became a new union—a second marriage.

Yes, we all have stories. We would be wise to consider the implications of sharing those stories with our progeny. It is only through prayer and a lot of soul searching that some stories should be shared, if at all. Certainly some parts of our stories need not be spoken; those choices are between us and God. But sometimes our stories are grand gifts, generational healers to be shared with those who come behind.

Yes, we all have stories. We are who we are, for better or worse, for richer or poorer, in sickness and in health, because of our stories.

PART 7

GRAND FINALE

THIRTY-SEVEN

SPIRITUAL OPPORTUNITIES

Always be prepared to give an answer to everyone who
asks you to give the reason for the hope that you have.
But do this with gentleness and respect.

—1 Peter 3:15

Life is full of opportunities for spiritual treasure. I have a
friend who says that every encounter is an opportunity for
prayer or blessing, and I believe her.

That is especially true for grandchildren. Every moment is
a moment to listen. Every second is an opportunity for teaching, instructing, modeling, or being present. Every conversation is a chance to marvel at God's creation and the miracle
of it all. A discussion of animals provides an opportunity to
share God's special provision and protection for every creature on earth. Reading a bedtime story provides an opportunity to discern truth from fiction.

As grandmothers we have the opportunity and the responsibility to make the most of these teachable moments. We never know when they are going to manifest themselves. I was reminded of this by my pastor in a sermon in which he told of a lighthouse off the east coast of Maine, built on a rock that was only exposed four hours a day due to the tides. The builders had a small window of opportunity in which to work on the lighthouse each day. That's how we are with our grandchildren. We are building that lighthouse. The only difference is that we never know when the rock will be exposed. We want to build a foundation at the moment the opportunity presents itself, and sometimes this is represented by a tiny window of time.

Last summer Jack visited us for a week of Vacation Bible School. One of his goals was to have a lemonade stand. He was determined to earn money to buy picture frames for his wildlife collection. One day, as we were sitting in temperatures above the century mark, I was not a happy camper with our arrangement. Up the street a crew was struggling in the heat, building a driveway. Jack immediately suggested that we market our wares. It hit me that this was a great opportunity to turn my own lemons into lemonade.

I told him that one of the most important things to me in life is to find a way to help others who are less fortunate. I suggested that we serve lemonade and cookies to the workmen as a gift of love, and I would donate their portion to his kitty. It warmed my heart to watch him as he served these men from his bounty with a loving spirit.

I began to wonder how many times a day I miss these spiritual opportunities with my family because of my focus on lemons rather than lemonade. How many times am I a hindrance, rather than an enhancer, in another's spiritual journey?

A few days later, the Lord gave me an example of this spiritual lesson. I was on the interstate, returning Jack to his home in Austin. The interstate between Fort Worth and Austin is a nightmare for the casual traveler and, more so, for a grandmother carrying such a precious cargo. Two lanes of traffic moving at seventy-five-plus miles per hour with concrete construction blocks over half the lanes don't do much for my confidence. Thank goodness the legislature has finally put up signs that say "left lane for passing only," but there are some who, out of carelessness or a rebellious heart, do not see or heed the instructions.

On this day, someone in a white Honda Accord was just such a driver. Going too slow in the left lane, her car blocked all the cars behind. Behind the wheel, a young girl on her cell phone was chatting away, blocking traffic for miles. She was probably not even aware. That's how we are, often unaware of our own actions and the impact they have on others.

At the same time, there was a driver in a pickup who was not happy at all about the Honda. He spent his time swerving in and out of the two lanes, causing havoc and near misses at every turn. Sometimes we are like this pickup. If we are not careful, we not only impede but also potentially can cause great destruction by our actions.

I love how Holly and Lee have chosen to be enhancers and not hindrances, taking advantage of opportunities to mentor their children about the importance of doing for others. Every spring and fall they all clean out their closets, choosing toys and clothes that are outgrown but still in good condition to give to the poor. At Christmas, they adopt a family, picking out special gifts just for them. Every week Holly takes a ninety-year-old lady from her church to the grocery store, with her three children in tow. Without words, her actions speak volumes, and the spiritual ramifications may affect generations to come.

Spiritual opportunities help build a foundation and a legacy for our grandchildren. A legacy has to start somewhere. Telling them things in a way that makes a difference can change lives. Being aware of daily opportunities as they manifest themselves can turn the tide in a child's life. My friend Janina is the best at recognizing spiritual opportunities and acting on them. I am learning from her how to better look and listen.

For now I am going to stay on point. Whenever I see a lemon, I am going to run, grab a pitcher, and head outside. For I know lemonade is just around the corner.

I'm going to be ready to catch the spiritual opportunities as they pour out in front of me.

THIRTY-EIGHT

THE INVISIBLE GIFT

Do not be afraid little flock, for your Father has been
pleased to give you the kingdom.
—Luke 12:32

M y grandson Jack recently turned six. When I called him
to ask what he wanted for his birthday, he told me: army
men, a tank, and Yu-Gi-Oh! cards. I'm always searching for a
gift that will please the honoree, so I opted for the army men
and tank per his request. When I e-mailed to thank him for
inviting me to his party, he e-mailed back this message:

Dear Marme. Thank you for coming to my party.

Next time you come I would like you to play with me with
my dartboard.

—LOVE, JACK

Jack's e-mail reinforces my belief that the perfect gift is not a material one. My grandchildren do not need nor do they want what I can give them; they need and want me. The best gift I can give them is me—my faith, wisdom, stories, morals, life lessons, and philosophy, not to mention my time and my presence.

I am most impressed with the many grandmothers whom I know who do special things and make special gifts for their grandchildren. Made by their own hands, these gifts of love are attached to forever memories.

My friend Bev hand smocks matching outfits for her grandchildren. The gift that they have now is a physical reminder of the love and care she feels for them. Courtney, who hardly remembers her grandparents at all, recently made a scrapbook for her granddaughter, Cameron. She included their memories and special times together. What a treasure for Cameron to keep long after Courtney is gone. Sylvia is teaching her grandchildren to play the piano. But more than that, she is introducing them to her world of music. She is giving them a gift they will always cherish. Jim and I plant trees at the ranch in honor of our grandchildren—living monuments representative of the life they have given us.

In the movie *Neverland*, the main character, author J. M

Barrie, creates a mixture of fantasy and reality in the lives and adventures of a family of four boys. He forms the ideas for Peter Pan as he plays their games of pirates and Indians. But the gift he gives is more important than the play he writes. The recipient is Peter, the young playwright, a child who is perhaps most wounded by the early death of his father. J. M. Barrie gives him more than a story; he validates and speaks truth to him, encouraging him to write his own stories. He gives the invisible gift.

My grandmother Maman took each of her granddaughters on a trip when they were twelve. It was not the trip that was important but the time spent together. From this experience, I have made a point to set aside special time with Jack, Lily, and James each time I visit them in Austin. It makes me remember the times my grandmother Shakey played Canasta with me. To this day I love the challenge, intimacy, and sense of order that come from playing cards.

My friend Carolyn spent the summer in Arkansas with her grandparents, gardening and learning to can vegetables. Today gardening is her therapy, passion, and time with the Lord. These gifts, although they are not seen by the naked eye, are not always identified by the giver or even the receiver as gifts. But they are gifts nevertheless.

The invisible gift comes in all shapes and sizes. Because

it comes out of the center of being, there is no clear way to recognize it. Nevertheless, it is a gift, always authentic, never manipulated nor contrived—a passion, a hobby, or a truth. Always it can be sharing our faith. It just comes out of who we are.

My grandson James loves hats, especially baseball hats worn backward. As the youngest child in his family, he rarely gets to be the boss. One of the invisible gifts I give to him is to let him be the boss of me. One of my favorite pictures is of him and me sitting at a soda fountain, eating ice cream, our baseball hats turned backward. I look like a complete fool, but the joy on his face is priceless.

Grandmothers are in the perfect position to give gifts that unlock life. These gifts may be invisible to others, but they are always visible to our grandchildren. What a perfect opportunity to breathe life upon a grandchild.

The invisible gift—I'll take it. Wrap up twenty for me, and make that to go!

THIRTY-NINE

SHEPHERDING GRANDCHILDREN

He tends his flock like a shepherd: He gathers the
lambs in his arms and carries them close to his heart.

—Isaiah 40:11

Until Strother was born, my grandson James was the youngest in the family. He is a little over two years old, and a more precious, lovable, good-natured child you will never find. This year he is starting preschool two mornings a week. Everyone loves James. He is great fun and such a peacemaker. Two weeks before school was to begin, out of the clear blue he announced that he was not going to school. "No tool," he said, and that was that.

Holly was a little concerned. As the third child, he had not attended Mother's Day Out and was not too pleased with Sunday school either. She saw a potential problem in the making.

That weekend, as providence would have it, he came to visit Big Dad and me—just him and us. What a grand time we had. We did all of his favorite things—went to the park, played with the trains, rode horses, visited the museum, ate ice cream, and had dinner at Luby's.

Sunday morning I decided that I would not alter my schedule. We would go to Sunday school. Looking in my storehouse of treasures, I found a white plastic backpack covered with yellow and blue ducks. We packed it with diapers, lotion, water, and goldfish, and off we went.

Someone later told me that they had never heard of a child carrying his own diapers, but my policy is if it works, don't fix it. He was so proud. He marched right into that building, announcing to everyone he saw, "Have backpack—my backpack!" I couldn't fail to see that this was a great opportunity to kill two birds with one stone. I was able to shepherd him yet at the same time help set the stage for a positive school experience.

I shared my experience with Lee and suggested they get him a new, special backpack. They did and called to inform me that the first day of school was a great success. He was so proud of his new backpack that he wore it all day, only to remove it for his bath. They had to peel it off of him after he fell asleep that night.

You see, we never know what action will result in success. We never know how God's wisdom and timing will undergird a situation. We never know when we might act as shepherds, making a difference in the lives of these little lambs.

I admit I do not know much about shepherding grandchildren, but I am learning. I was not too strong in this area when my kids were young. I never taught Sunday school or Vacation Bible School. It is only recently that I have been volunteering in the Sunday school nursery as a substitute. I love what open doors these kids are, how they hang on to every word I say or sing. I delight in their wonder and joy. No wonder Jesus tells us to come to him as little children.

I do see some progress from my past, however. Today, I am bolder with my grandchildren than I was with my own children. We pray aloud, and I am not afraid to share my faith with them or talk about God. One day when Jack was about four, we were riding in the car. All of a sudden, I heard this small voice pipe up from the back seat. He began to tell me that his friend Grace told him that he was supposed to ask Jesus into his heart, but he didn't want to. Did he have to? I was able to tell him that his decision was okay, but Jesus wanted to come into his heart, and he would wait until Jack was ready to ask him. This opened up a whole avenue of discussion—an opportunity for shepherding that just presented itself before me.

One of my most tender moments and confirmation that shepherding, indeed, is going on in spite of myself came as I was putting James to bed that same backpack Sunday. We were singing songs and had sung "Row Da Boat" one hundred times. I prayed with him and then asked him what song he wanted me to sing. He looked up at me with those beautiful blue eyes and said, "Sing, 'Jesus.'" It took me a moment to shift gears. I remembered that when he was a baby, I used to rock him to sleep. I have a soft music-box lamb that plays "Jesus Loves Me" over and over, and I would sing that to him as I rubbed his back. It had been a long time, yet he remembered.

Shepherding grandchildren is a huge responsibility. Leading them to green pastures is an honor and privilege. Who would exchange it for gold and silver? Not I, not in a hundred years.

FORTY

CROSSING THE RIVER

There will be no more death or mourning or crying or
pain, for the old order of things has passed away.
—Revelation 21:4

In today's world, rural America is an anomaly. Anyone who has not had an occasion to spend time there is missing out. If I hadn't married into it, I would have missed it myself.

In the country, Sunday lunch is a big deal. After the last bite of pecan pie, everyone rises from the table as the patriarch of the family announces, "It's time to go across the river." Jim's father did it for sixty years, crossing the Brazos to the family ranch.

Going across the river can be loosely defined as hopping in the pickup to ride the fence line, taking inventory of the property. Conversation revolves around what has been done, what needs to be done, or what ought to be done. Going across the river occurs every day, usually following a meal, but it can also be done in the morning or late evening. No explanation is needed. Everyone in our family knows what "going across the river" means.

Jim's dad died on November 30, 2006. He was the last of his line. No one thought he would outlive them all, though in retrospect we can see that he was the strongest one. The patriarch, a man of his time, finally gathered to his people.

It was a peaceful passing. In typical Weldon style, he made a dry run two weeks before, but he fooled us all by making a quick recovery. I suspect that he needed time to prepare himself spiritually for his leave-taking. In those two weeks, he talked about his wife, whom he had not mentioned since his dementia kicked in three months after her death. He began looking to the church. He spoke of God.

We were cautious when he took to his bed that Sunday. This time he did not get up, and he died on a Wednesday night. He left big shoes to fill and a legacy that will touch generations.

We met to take him home—to the land he loved. We were blessed to accompany him on this, his final journey across the river.

It was the coldest day of the year. Wouldn't you know it? The furnace placed in the family home many years before died on the same day. One couldn't help but wonder if this was not a sign of the fire of this simple but mighty man going out.

We gathered in the cold house. Our hearts were warm as family and a smattering of friends and contemporaries joined forces to bring him home. I was surprised at the rush of tears when I greeted his few remaining friends. I could see that it was truly the end of an era.

Lee gave the eulogy. How proud I was as he stood there, namesake of his father and grandfather. I sat next to Jack (John Lee), the namesake of them all. What a wonderful tribute he gave as he spoke of the lessons learned at his grandfather's feet. In poetic form, he beautifully described the years they spent crossing the river together:

As a child, farm implements became warriors;
Tree houses were mansions, and horses were toys.
The tank was for skinny dipping on really hot days,
And riding three wheelers was only allowed on the ranch
    for young boys.
As I grew I became more aware,
My days were filled with campfire stories and folklore . . .
Information and lessons were passed on too,
Spurred by the wisdom of another . . . I wanted to know
    more.

I learned of a strong work ethic, and the ability to laugh.
Tales of an elder's childhood and stories of World War II
were told.
I learned of economics, of Indians, of death and the past.
I learned the lessons from experience, not mine, but from
long gone men of old.
My lessons varied depending on what took us "across the
river."

In those forty-five minutes, the torch was passed from Lee Weldon to James Lee Sr. to James Lee Jr. down to John Lee, the fourth generation. I couldn't help but marvel at the miracle of God's timing. We had captured the passing of this torch in picture form just one week prior. At Darin's urging, the four generations spent Thanksgiving afternoon with their grand-dad, not knowing of his soon homegoing.

In spite of the sadness, there were amazing moments of spiritual clarity. Lily and Jack had a natural curiosity. "Is Grand-dad in heaven with Jesus?" Lily asked as she swaddled her baby doll, mimicking Blythe and Strother.

"Yes," I replied, "he is. And he's with Grandmother too."

"Can he talk?" she asked.

"Yes, I suppose he can. Right now, he might be talking with Jesus or Grandmother, but we can't hear him."

"Is Grandad in that box?" she asked at the cemetery.

"Yes, his body is in that box, but his spirit is already with God," I answered. "It's important that we stand here and show him honor as we bring him to his final home."

For the first time I realized the significance of taking someone home. My father-in-law has returned home. He is now with his people, at peace, at rest. He has made his final trip across the river. It is the end of an era.

Going across the river has taken on new meaning for me. Life will never be the same again.

FORTY-ONE

GOING OUT IN STYLE

This is what the kingdom of heaven is like. A man
scatters seed on the ground. Night and day, whether
he sleeps or gets up, the seed sprouts and grows,
though he does not know how. All by itself the soil
produces grain—first the stalk, then the head, then the
full kernel in the head.

—Mark 4:26–28

Everyone wants to leave a legacy. I know I do. Life is a
moment in time that will be remembered after our time
on this earth is completed.

My mother tells a great story about her mother-in-law
Helen, Guppy's mother. A few weeks after Helen died, my
mother went over to her house to begin the process of cleaning out. When she opened the first linen cabinet, she had the
shock of her life. Everything was folded neatly, stacked, color

coordinated, ironed, and in place. Every sheet, towel, and pillowcase was in perfect shape. It appeared as if someone had just moved in and was arranging a new house.

Every cabinet was the same—cleaned out, junk removed, orderly, and in place.

As she was pondering this phenomenon, Grace, Helen's next-door neighbor, walked in the back door. She proceeded to relate a story that happened six months before Helen's death. Grace had come by for a cup of coffee, and she found Helen on her hands and knees, cleaning out the pantry, laughing to herself.

"Grace, look at this," she chuckled, "can you imagine the surprise on Cecca's face when she opens these doors?"

Helen went out in style. She was prepared. She got her house in order, literally and physically.

Before I go, that is what I want to do: get my house in order.

I am talking not only about my physical house, but I am talking also about my spiritual, emotional, and psychological houses. I want to get them all in order. I want to remove the junk, the baggage, the worn and torn—clean them out, reorder, replace so that when I am gone, nothing remains undone. If there are no regrets, no unspoken words of forgiveness, no grudges, no unresolved issues, if I could leave a clean slate as part of my legacy—what a gift that would be.

More importantly, this cleaning out of my house is planting seeds for my children and grandchildren. Rather than concentrating on regrets, they will remember all of the good things: the joy, laughter, and hope—the life that I carried inside of me.

At my last breath, I hope they think I breathed life upon their world, that in everything I touched, in everything I did, I brought life and healing rather than death and despair. I hope that my presence planted a garden in their lives.

Darin and Blythe recently bought a new house. They moved in February, in the dead of winter. In the middle of March, they had an unexpected surprise. Everywhere, new life began to push forth from the ground, each day yielding a new-found discovery, a new growth to anticipate and ponder. Every day they would call to tell me about a new treasure they had discovered. Each call was full of excitement and anticipation. It was clear that someone had lovingly and carefully planted a garden of life, and it was beginning to show itself long after the time of sowing.

I want to plant a garden of life, a garden of surprises. After I am gone, I want my loved ones to discover new growth, new surprises, new wonders, new gems that I have left behind. I want them to do nothing but sit and watch, to tend that which was already planted. I want them to appreciate a garden that has already been weeded and fertilized, composted with a covering of protection, cultivated by loving hands.

Yes, I want to go out in style. Right now, I have a lot of baggage and weeds in my house and in my garden. But I'm ready to start clearing out the clutter!

What am I going to do with the rest of my life? I am going to weed the garden that I am sowing. I am going to prepare the soil, gather the seed, plant and fertilize, water and tend. I am going to clean out the closets of my life, unearth the dross in hidden places, and discard that which I have held on to for too long. I am going to get my house in order.

Going out in style? You bet I am.

FORTY-TWO

THE POWER OF ONE

I declare your power to the next generation, your might
to all who are to come.
—Psalm 71:18

The power of one—the impact of one word, one voice, one person, one action—can have a profound effect on a life forever.

A few years ago, Jim and I went to see a movie titled *The Power of One*. A true story about one man's impact on apartheid in the boxing world in South Africa, I was moved to tears by its powerful message. At the end of the movie, I looked around to see that there were only five people in the whole theater. I couldn't believe my eyes. Where were the people? They had missed the opportunity to experience the power of one.

The next night we went to see *Basic Instinct* with Michael Douglas and Sharon Stone, and there was standing room only. Then I understood—here is where the people are. I was astonished. The message of love and commitment was totally distorted. I vowed then and there that I would exercise the power of one. I announced that I was now boycotting violent movies and those with explicit sex scenes. I don't believe my one-woman stand made a dent in the profit of Universal Pictures, but it certainly made me feel better. I doubt if it changed anyone's mind, but at least people knew where I stood.

I know it made an impact on my sons. To this day, they still call to say, "Mom, I have a movie for you to boycott." The power of one.

In 1996, I went on a mission trip to Malawi, Central Africa. There were twelve on our team, and we went to initiate a relationship between our diocese and the diocese of Northern Malawi. It was a life-changing experience. When we returned, we had no idea what seeds had been planted, what might be harvested in the future. It is only now, ten years later, that we are beginning to see the fruit of that trip. Though there were twelve of us, we were united by the banner of love with one message. We moved together as one, and lives were changed.

The power of one can either be used for good or as an instrument for evil. It is important to be aware of the opposing influences and act accordingly. Unintended consequences are always a byproduct of any action and thus should be weighed carefully.

In the movie *Grand Canyon*, there is a great scene where the top movie mogul becomes a victim of a violent crime. The irony is not lost on the audience, as his main production focus was on violent movies. He justified his actions by stating that his movies reflected society, not influenced it. After his mugging he had an epiphany, seeing the error of his ways. For a few weeks he planned the positive message he would carry to the world. His transformation was short-lived, however. At the end of the movie, he is seen riding a golf cart toward his studio. He enters a dark, cavernous building, returning to the darkness as he defends his return to violence. The significance of this scene of a lost and dark world cannot be missed.

Contrast that with a real life power of one—Oprah. One cannot help but respect what she has done with her life, for she has the ability to affect millions. She has taken on topics and controversies, impacting and changing the world for good. I remember the moment she realized the potential impact of her show, vowing to promote good and not highlight evil. To her credit, she has been true to her calling. The Oprah Winfrey Academy of Leadership will change the face of women in Africa. The significance of its placement in South Africa is not lost on this writer. The world will be forever changed. The power of one—do not underestimate its value.

There are many inspiring stories about people who have succeeded against all odds and who have used the power of one for good. Annie Sullivan and her impact on the hearing impaired, as she worked with Helen Keller, changed the way the world dealt with the deaf—the power of one.

Billy Graham and his worldwide evangelism have changed the world for Christ. He has gone to the ends of the earth to spread the gospel. Lives have been changed and families have been transformed—the power of one.

Jim Elliot and Nate Saint gave their lives to follow the call to evangelize the Auca Indians. Years later, Nate's son Steve returned to that same tribe and forgave the man who had murdered his father. Today that tribe is a testament to the power of one. The belief in the One who transforms has changed an entire people group.

Grandmothers also have the opportunity to be the power of one in the lives of grandchildren. If we stay connected to God, stay true to our values, share our faith, and show integrity and kindness in everything we do, we can be encouragers and inspirers of a new generation.

Many years ago, Peter, Paul, and Mary did a Christmas TV special. In their typical energized and emotional style, they sang a song titled "Light One Candle." Starting with a dark stage, one young boy walked from the back of the stage, carrying a tiny candle. His light began to shine, and the dark was punctured by a small ray of light. As his candle touched the candles near him, the entire auditorium was awash with light and unity.

I want to be that one who lights that first candle, who brings light and unity into a dark auditorium, into a dark world. I want to be that one who touches my light to my grandchild's light. I would hope that his light would touch another—and the world would be a better place.

I want to make a difference. I want my brief time on earth to count—if only for a moment in time—to take the power of One who lights the world and become a power of one that makes a difference for eternity.

ABOUT THE AUTHOR

Marty Norman is a freelance writer, licensed therapist with a master's in education from Southwestern Seminary, workshop trainer, inspirational speaker, mother of two, and grandmother of four. She is a founding member of the First Grandmother's Club, an organization dedicated to serving underprivileged children through volunteerism, donations, and projects. She also cofounded Grandmother Connections, an educational partnership that offers grandparenting seminars.

Marty worked in individual practice for ten years as a therapist as well as a counselor and volunteer for nonprofit family-service organizations. She has taught seminars on family dynamics, communication, image consulting, career development, and conflict management. She also introduced Project Charlie, a drug prevention curriculum for fifth graders, into the Fort Worth Independent School District. Her special areas of expertise are art therapy and journaling for therapeutic healing. Her other specialties include women's issues, drug and alcohol addiction, sexual abuse, grief issues, and play therapy for children.

She and her husband, Jim, live in Fort Worth, Texas, where she loves to hike, garden, oil paint, and read but mostly play with her grandkids.

For more information, please visit
www.firstgrandmothersclub.org